D0881860

DARING TO BE UNITED

Including Lesbians and Gays in The United Church of Canada

Alyson C. Huntly

UNITED CHURCH PUBLISHING HOUSE

TORONTO, CANADA

Daring to Be United: Including Lesbians and Gays in The United Church of Canada

Copyright © 1998 United Church Publishing House

All rights reserved. No part of this book may be photocopied, reproduced, stored in a retrieval system, or transmitted, in any form or by any means, electronic, mechanical or otherwise, without the written permission of the United Church Publishing House.

All biblical quotations, unless otherwise noted, are from the *New Revised Standard Version Bible*, copyright © 1989, by the Division of Christian Education of the National Council of the Churches of Christ in the United States of America.

Canadian Cataloguing in Publication Data

Huntly, Alyson
  Daring to be united : including lesbians and gays in the United Church of Canada

Includes bibliographical references and index
ISBN 1-55134-082-8

1. Homosexuality — Religious aspects — United Church of Canada.
2. Ordination of gays — United Church of Canada.   I. Title.

BX9881.H86 1998   261.8'35766'08827   C98-930864-2

United Church Publishing House
3250 Bloor Street West
Etobicoke, Ontario
Canada M8X 2Y4
416-231-5931
bookpub@uccan.org
www.uccan.org/ucph/home.htm

Design and Production: Department of Publishing and Graphics
Cover art: *Internal Landscape* by Laura Ciruls

Printed in Canada

 980078

TO RUTH

To Ruth and all women
who have loved a woman
with fierce loyalty or tender pride,
with great courage and against all odds,
risking their reputation, their jobs,
their friends, their family, even their lives
to Ruth and all those who have put love before security,
refusing to be bound by the fetters of law or fear or convention,
who by their daring have created new paths in wild places
to Ruth and all women who love women
I say thank you.

To Boaz and all men
who have challenged sexual oppression
by speaking out, taking responsibility,
calling others to account, changing their language
and their behaviour,
creating safe space, sharing power
to Boaz, and all those who have protected the vulnerable,
welcomed the outcast, shared bread,
given shelter, stood vigil, written letters,
spoken out, stood to be counted
to Boaz and all those who have worked
to make this world tender and more just
I say thank you.

To Naomi and all those
who have dared to ask
for what they are entitled to,
who have refused to be ignored
or turned back or passive or victims,
who by their persistent belief
that justice is not only right but possible
have halted armies, changed structures,
saved forests, fed children
to Naomi and all people who have demonstrated justice
I say thank you.

To Naomi, Boaz, Ruth and all those
who have chosen to be family,
who have adopted children,
loved someone of their own gender,
liked their in-laws,
formed unusual alliances and unlikely friendships,
created community, nurtured hope,
befriended themselves and one another,
to Naomi, Boaz, Ruth and all those who have discovered
that community is not built like a wall but grown like a garden
and have chosen to tend that garden,
seen one another through, wept, listened,
plotted and made possible
knowing that family is, in the largest sense,
a choice and a gift
to Naomi and all those who have chosen to be family
I say thank you.

CONTENTS

FOREWORD

I n the spring of 1997 I was asked to provide leadership for an event entitled "Spirituality for the Long Haul" sponsored by the Church and Society Committee of Ottawa Presbytery. Because the invitation had included the request that I be quite personal in my examples, I had identified four specific times in my life when I faced a "long haul" and I shared what had helped me meet the challenge. It will come as no surprise to those who read this book that I identified as the "longest haul" my involvement in the sexual orientation debate.

I told how I had entered into the debate first in 1980 in Ottawa Presbytery when we, the members of the Education and Student Committee, had been warned that we might have a gay candidate, and were asked how we intended to respond. I refused to "vote" without a study of the issue, and offered to organize a retreat for committee members and commissioners to General Council. We spent a weekend looking at biblical, theological, medical and social questions. In the end we decided that there was no reason for withholding ordination on the basis of sexual orientation alone, but we added the rider that we were not sure the church was ready for such a decision without further study. I was naïve enough at that time to think that anyone who did the same study would come to the same conclusion. How wrong I was! Especially about people doing the study! But we did address the issue at the 1980 General Council when it was raised as part of the report, "In God's Image. Male and Female: A Study on Human Sexuality."

I inherited the issue when I joined the Division of Ministry Personnel and Education (MP&E) as general secretary in 1982, and in 1984 our report came to the same conclusion. The church was still not ready to move and mandated another study. The second study, published in 1988, went even further in support and the howls of rage were even stronger. By this time I was Moderator (1986-88) and intimately involved in the issue. Those eight years were a long haul indeed.

There were three things that helped me survive the hate mail, the obscene telephone calls, the threats, the insults, the foul language, the media attention and the pressure to take the issue off the General Council agenda. First of all, I had read extensively and I was very sure of my position. Secondly, in the long hours I spent in prayer, I always emerged feeling held and affirmed. And thirdly, I knew that I had the support of many people who were there for me when I needed them. Over the long haul I became convinced that I was where I was because God had chosen me to be there.

In preparation for this book, Alyson Huntly has interviewed many people whose lives were affected intimately by the sexual orientation debate. In this foreword, I add my own reflections. I appreciate Alyson's careful analysis and her sympathetic hearing of the stories others have told, and I know that "out there" there are many untold stories of courage and disillusion, success and disappointment, homophobia and support.

During my time at MP&E my role required that I support the work of its committees, and to spread the word of what was being recommended. This I did wholeheartedly because I believed in what the report was saying. When I was Moderator I was torn by two different responsibilities: one to give spiritual leadership, which to me meant spreading the word about inclusivity and openness, and another to listen to the church and to report to the General Council Executive what I was hearing. Much of what I was hearing was an anathema to me. I solved the dilemma by listening but at the same time questioning, and sharing what others were telling me.

When my term as Moderator was over, I returned home ready to forget, for a time at least, the whole question of sexual orientation and ordination. But I was not really prepared for the silence that met me. No one wanted to discuss the issue, and in time this became a burden for me. My own congregation refused to become involved in any further debate, even though many of us would have supported becoming an Affirming Congregation. Too many felt that there had been division enough and were hesitant about opening old wounds. Added to this was the realization that my journey with cancer would not let me take the initiative; I simply did not have the energy.

One of my great delights once the cancer was once again under control was to be invited to preach at the service in which Trinity-St. Paul's United in Toronto became an Affirming Congregation. One point that I made was that truth, however painful, must be faced because it is only in honest descriptions of a sickness that needs curing that prescriptions for a cure can be developed. In the case of homosexuality, the sickness is in attitudes toward it, not the sexual orientation itself.

I quoted Douglas Hall, who insists that we do not have the truth to tell. A truth cannot be had; it must be lived with, stood under, not just understood, because this truth is not an it but a Thou. It is not words but The Word. And even if we cannot possess it we must make bold to become its witnesses in the world. That is why it is not enough to passively accept the ruling of General Council in the name of justice. What is required is righteousness, that ever-flowing stream that demands action, demands change, initiates change.

With God's grace, this book will help us all move in that direction.

Anne Squire

ACKNOWLEDGEMENTS

In the course of writing this book I travelled to many parts of Canada. I was welcomed and invited into people's lives in ways I would never have imagined. I am honoured by the trust placed in me, and grateful for all the many signs of welcome and support I received along the way—a bed for the night, coffee for the road, a bright yellow Volvo to drive across the Prairies, helpful suggestions, friendly advice and, above all, the outpouring of stories. There are far too many individuals to thank by name. I hope that the pages that follow can attest to my deep gratitude.

For every story included in this book there are others, equally compelling, that also could be told. There are many people who talked with me whose exact words and experiences do not appear here. But their shared stories have shaped very deeply my understanding of this passage in our church's life, and I am grateful for those many wonderful conversations.

Jenni Huntly offered her research talents, checking facts and statistics. D'thea Webster gave invaluable feedback and helped with manuscript preparation. My thanks to you both.

Joan Hibbard's story was adapted from an article she wrote for *Together in Faith: Inclusive Resources about Sexual Diversity, for Study, Dialogue and Action*, the Division of Mission in Canada, The United Church of Canada, 1995. It is used with permission.

The words by Sylvia Dunstan that appear at the beginning of Chapter 2 are used with the permission of her estate. The first part of the story about "Clare" in Chapter 6 was written by the person whose experience this is. The anecdote about graffiti on someone's car that begins Chapter 17 was written by the person whose experience this is, and was originally published in *Consensus*. It is used with permission.

Thanks to Ron Coughlin and David Hallman for making available archival material and documents, and to Loraine MacKenzie Shepherd for giving such ready access to her own research and articles. Thanks to the many others who supplied current and historical documents.

I owe a special debt of gratitude to Affirm United for the help that it gave me: making suggestions for contacts, supporting the project, getting the word out and above all in trusting me in this endeavour. Affirm United has been at the forefront of the struggle for sexual inclusivity in the United Church, and without the commitment and courage of its members this story could not be written.

I would like to thank the staff of the United Church Publishing House for believing that this was a story worth telling.

My family and friends stuck by me, as I became more and more entangled in this project. I thank you for your love and encouragement. Thanks to Crystal, Michael and Rachael for being family, respecting my work and tolerating my preoccupation. You continue to be a source of hope, deep joy and a lifeline to the world.

With my love and thanks,

Alyson Huntly
January 1998

WORDS TO BEGIN

All experience is an arch to build upon.

Henry Brook Adams

In 1988 the United Church decided not to exclude people from ministry on the basis of their sexual orientation. The 10 or so years leading up to that decision were years of intense struggle and turmoil. The aftershocks were even more immense. Giving to the national church's Mission and Service Fund dropped in 1988, although it recovered the next year. Some members left certain congregations to join others where they felt more at home; some people left the United Church altogether. Many congregations, presbyteries and Conferences were deeply and bitterly divided. Some friendships were lost in the process, as people encountered radically different opinions and decisions. Then slowly, piece by piece, the United Church picked up and moved on.

For some, moving on meant not talking any more about an issue that had been so divisive and painful. It was, and may still be, true that the majority of United Church members were not in complete agreement with the decisions their elected representatives made at the General Councils in 1988 and 1990. Perhaps some people were willing to put up with this particular decision because the United Church meant more to them than this one issue. They didn't want to talk about it any more and they certainly hoped it would never touch their home congregation, but they were willing to get on with the business of being the church.

Some said that nothing had really changed; the church had simply dared to be what it already was—an inclusive and open denomination. In fact, there really was no substantial change in 1988, on paper at any rate. General

Council had only upheld existing United Church policy, since there never had been criteria for excluding any groups of persons from membership. A conscious decision not to exclude, however, is ultimately a decision to include. A door had been opened, if only by a crack. Or, as one person said at the time, "at least it hadn't been locked, chained, and bolted shut." The United Church had changed.

The changes that began long before that historic moment in 1988 have continued. Sometimes change has been spectacular and most surprising. More often it has been very small, very slow, very subtle. It is only in retrospect that one sees how different things really are. For everywhere, even in the most unlikely parts of the church, there are signs of greater tolerance, acceptance and inclusion of people of different sexual orientations.

This book shares some of those stories of change. It uses people's own words and experiences to tell of congregations, church structures and individual lives that have been transformed, and to identify some of the elements that made change possible. These stories are, of course, not the whole picture. There are many places in our church where gay, lesbian and bisexual people are still excluded, where the issues are not talked about, or where nothing has changed. But these stories are told to show what is happening in some parts of the church, and what might be possible in other places.

No one story can capture the essence of The United Church of Canada. Like snapshots in a family album, stories preserve a glimpse of a moment in time. Even a large collection of stories cannot give the whole picture of a church as diverse and complex as this one. The stories told in this book have been primarily ones of hope, occasions in which change, however small, is apparent. They show people changing their hearts and minds, people committed to a vision of inclusion and justice, and gays and lesbians being welcomed, accepted and valued.

There are other facets of the United Church's ongoing struggle with this issue. More than 30 years after the first woman was ordained in the United Church there are still some congregations that resist the idea of women in ministry. So there are certainly a great many where gay and lesbian clergy would not yet be welcome! Even with an official policy of inclusion, most gay and lesbian clergy and students are not ready to risk coming out in their congregations. The homophobia of Canadian society spills over into our churches, and many gay and lesbian lay people still feel unwelcome or invisible.

Nevertheless, these stories of hope and change are true. They are part of the fabric and essence of The United Church of Canada. They are indicators of who we are as a church, at this time, while pointing to where we might be in the future. They offer hope that change is possible by showing us what the church looks like when an inclusive vision takes root. They offer an ongoing challenge to the rest of the church, and to the world. They give us images of God's welcoming and unconditional love.

There are many stories that do not appear in this book. Some people chose to leave The United Church of Canada in or around 1988. For some of them, this difficult choice came because they could not live with the decision that had been made not to exclude gay and lesbian people from ministry. They believed homosexuality was sinful and against biblical teaching. They felt the United Church was on the wrong path. For some it was this one issue alone around which they felt called to make this move. For others the issue was the final straw in a long list of concerns around which they felt a strong sense of discord with the United Church's position and faith stance. Many chose to leave, I believe, because out of their own deeply held sense of faith and faithfulness, they could no longer find a spiritual home within the United Church. In many cases, this was a decision made prayerfully and after much struggle. Often it was deeply painful.

Other people left the United Church for different yet parallel reasons. There were candidates whose call had been turned down solely on the basis of their sexual orientation. There were lay people who had begun to declare their sexual orientation, only to feel shunned or silenced. There were closeted gay and lesbian clergy who felt that, even after 1988, there was still no real affirmation for them and their gifts. Many gay, lesbian and bisexual people had felt the pain of exclusion for so many years that the 1988 decision was simply not enough to keep them in the church. For some it didn't go far enough. For others it came too late and after too much pain.

I am conscious of the void that is left in our church, and in this book, by those who left. Their absence is keenly felt. I respect the choices made, however, for I believe that they were made carefully and in faith. I pray that God will continue to bless all of our journeys. I continue to believe that God can and will one day make of our human discord and disunity a oneness forged in Christ's Spirit. I hope that God will continue to build of our human institutions a church that dares to live out God's inclusive and uniting love.

1

THE ISSUE YEARS

As you walk, you cut open and create the riverbed into which the stream of your descendants shall enter and flow.

Nikos Kazantzakis

[T]he church is an anvil which has worn out many hammers.

James R. Mutchmor

Anne Squire was elected Moderator of the United Church in 1986, launching her into the heart of the United Church's struggles with The Issue, the term that came to be used to describe the whole discussion of homosexuality. Squire was just finishing her term as Moderator at the 1988 General Council in Victoria. At one point, she took a break from the plenary floor and went out into the lobby. "I have this very vivid memory of taking a glass of pink lemonade from the display table Affirm had set up," she said. Affirm was an organization of United Church gays, lesbians and bisexuals. She then went over to the woman siting at the registration table. "I hadn't yet had a chance to thank her for all the hard work she was doing," Squire said. The woman told Squire she had come to the General Council completely against the ordination of gays and lesbians. When she saw Affirm set up its table with the pink lemonade stand, she was very upset.

She never heard a word of the debate, her view of the proceedings limited, as it was, to the hallway outside the Council meeting space. But the registration table was near Affirm's information table. She watched its members interacting with Council delegates. "I've been watching them," the woman said of Affirm. "They're the friendliest group in the whole lobby. I've changed my mind."

❦

The window of Mabel Christie's condominium apartment looks out over the trees and roof-tops of a quiet Ottawa neighbourhood. Trinity United Church is just around the corner. It's the summer of 1997. A small group of church friends has gathered in her living room to talk, once again, about The Issue. Most of the group are in their seventies. Christie herself is 86.

As she bustles about with teacups and plates of homemade cookies, she is anxious to make her guests feel at home, and itching to get into the conversation. She finds herself slowing down a little these days, but she still has lots of passion and energy when it comes to talking about homosexuality, the church and ministry. Putting down the teapot, she recalls an incident at presbytery in the spring of 1988. It is something that still exasperates her. Someone asked for a show of hands from those who had read the document being discussed, "Toward a Christian Understanding of Sexual Orientations, Lifestyles and Ministry." Most people admitted that they hadn't read it. Then someone stood up and announced that although he hadn't looked at it, he was against it anyway. "So many times we make judgements when we don't know what we're talking about," Christie declares. The others nod in agreement.

Those gathered in Christie's apartment did take seriously the need to study and reflect on The Issue. They began to read and talk and listen back in the early '80s when the United Church released one of its early study documents, "In God's Image. Male and Female: A Study on Human Sexuality." Most of them were more than 60 at the time, and not from a generation used to talking about sex, especially not in church. For Doreen Armstrong it was the first time she had ever sat in a group discussing human sexuality, marriage, heterosexuality and homosexuality. "It was quite interesting," she recalls. The others laugh. Interesting may not be quite the right word for it. Sex and sexuality just weren't mentioned in church in those days. Most of the group had never met someone they knew to be homosexual. Most had never thought much about it.

Now it's more commonplace, more visible. The issue of homosexuality has touched their lives more directly through the lives of their children, grandchildren and friends. At the time, though, no one would have talked about things like that.

"I was pretty dumb about the whole issue," says Alex McKeague, recalling the time members of the study group invited a gay couple to come and talk with them. "Here were these nice people saying how they'd come to accept the way they were," he explains. That personal encounter made all the difference. It was a pivotal moment for Alex and his wife, Jane McKeague.

"I guess all of us graduated from the experience as more tolerant people," says Jane. "It's a justice issue," adds Alex.

Similar discussions were happening right across the United Church in the 1980s in churches big and small, rural and urban. Not everyone came to the same conclusion as Christie and her friends. Even at Trinity United in Ottawa, when it came to the issue of sexual orientation and ministry, there was deep division.

Trinity United called a meeting in April 1988 to allow members to voice their opinions on the recommendations that would be going that summer to the General Council, the United Church's highest elected decision-making body. Doreen Armstrong took the minutes. She still has the notes. Out of a congregational membership of 500, nearly 200 people showed up for a day of discussion. At the end of the day, the votes were tallied. Seventy per cent of those who gathered agreed with the statement, "We affirm the acceptance of all human beings as persons made in the image of God, regardless of their sexual orientation." But on the key recommendation that sexual orientation should not be a barrier to participation in the order of ministry, 66 per cent were opposed. That number was pretty typical of the United Church as a whole. When *The United Church Observer* commissioned a survey of United Church members in 1988, it found that 65 per cent thought homosexuals shouldn't be ordained.

The study document that Christie and her group worked through together, "In God's Image..," was one of a series of reports and study documents prepared by the United Church dealing with issues of human sexuality. In 1972, the General Council agreed to carry out a comprehensive study of human sexuality, but for various reasons it wasn't until 1978 that a task group met to prepare a report. The document they wrote, "In God's Image...," was accepted as a study document by the 1980 General Council and circulated to the wider church for discussion and reflection. It wasn't primarily about sexual orientation or about ministry. It focused broadly on issues of sexuality, marriage and family. The impetus for this focus on sexuality was a growing concern about marriage and family breakdown, changing roles of women and men in society, feminism, inclusive language, gender roles and a growing awareness of injustice and violence against women. The issue of homosexuality and eligibility for ministry had not yet begun to surface as a major issue in the church. It was, in many ways, only a minor comment in a much larger document.

The Rev. Pierre Goldberger is principal of United Theological College in Montreal. He notes that the issue of homosexuality and ministry was really only a subset of a much broader discussion about roles and relationships. "'In God's Image. Male and Female' was a telling title," he reflects. "We were addressing a whole range of issues—theology, the Bible and, of course, sexuality. And one of the footnotes of the debate was discussion of the variety of sexual orientations that exist." Thus an issue that was initially quite peripheral to the conversation took on a life of its own. This "by the way" took on a whole new dimension, and became the focus for a whole lot of unresolved issues within the United Church.

It wasn't an issue that most people would have chosen as a focus for the church's energy and life for more than a decade. But it came to be the focal point around which the United Church was forced to make decisions, and to decide who it was, and who it was to become as The United Church of Canada. Goldberger admits he initially resisted this issue becoming such a central focus of energy, and yet he came to see it as a confessional issue. "At certain times, the breadth and depth and courage of our faith is tested in certain historical rendezvous that we don't always control," he says. "This issue was one. This was how the integrity of our church was tested—were we going to come out into the 21st century plural and inclusive?" The question became: Was the church going to be true to who it was as The United Church of Canada?

"In God's Image..." acknowledged that there were already gay ministers in the United Church, as there were in every denomination, and it recommended that "there is no reason in principle why mature, self-accepting homosexuals ... should not be ordained or commissioned."

This was only a line in a study document, but it was enough to set the alarm bells sounding. Clearly, the United Church as a whole was not yet ready to make such a statement. Several more study processes were initiated. In the meantime, however, several gay and lesbian candidates for ministry had either told the committees responsible for deciding on their candidacy that they were homosexual, or had been identified by others as being homosexual. In 1982, Hamilton Conference refused to ordain an openly lesbian woman. It went on to develop a policy statement that the Conference would not ordain or commission any "self-declared" homosexual, and called on the national church to enact a church-wide policy.

Other Conferences faced with similar dilemmas also asked the national church for a policy statement. A task group was formed to prepare a report.

In February 1984, the Division of Ministry Personnel and Education studied a task group report entitled "Sexual Orientation and Eligibility for the Order of Ministry" and approved its principal recommendation that "in and of itself, sexual orientation should not be a factor in determining membership in the order of ministry of The United Church of Canada." The full report was to be acted on by the upcoming General Council in Morden, Manitoba, that summer. It was circulated as an insert in the April 1984 issue of *The United Church Observer.* Thus some 290,000 United Church households received a report that recommended ordination for gay and lesbian people. There was an immediate furor. The media had a heyday.

If there is such a thing as a typical United Church member, it would be someone like Daphne Craig. She trained as a teacher after finishing high school, but is long since retired. She has lived most of her life in rural Ontario, attending a small, rural church. The people in her church are very friendly. Members are quick to care for one another if someone needs a helping hand. It's also quite conservative when it comes to issues of sexuality. It was a big deal when, in 1996, the church called its first female minister.

Craig has been active on many church committees, both within her local congregation and at other levels of the church. In 1984, she was elected a commissioner (elected delegate) to the General Council in Morden. Commissioners were asked to choose a "Manitoba Experience" for the weekend in the middle of the Council. One option, "The Hidden Christians," was hosted by a gay and lesbian church in Winnipeg. It intrigued Craig, because she knew nothing about the subject. Until then, she'd led what she describes as "an extremely sheltered life" and had never encountered or discussed homosexuality. She was introduced to her hosts for the weekend, a lesbian couple. First on the itinerary was a gay rights demonstration at the provincial legislature.

Craig took an instant liking to her hosts. They talked late into the evening. On Sunday morning they worshipped together in a church whose primary ministry is with gay and lesbian people. "I heard the pain of so many who were treated as pariahs because they did not follow the norm in their loving," she says. The weekend changed forever Craig's opinions. Back home, she couldn't stop talking about her experience, and what she learned.

She's still trying to explain, in a congregation where most people disagree with her to this day.

The 1984 General Council adopted recommendations from the report that urged an end to discrimination against homosexual persons, "towards full civil and human rights in society." The Council also acknowledged that, throughout its history, the church had condoned and even encouraged the rejection and persecution of homosexual persons. But the issue of ministry, particularly ordained ministry, remained unresolved. The Council concluded that further study was needed, and postponed the decision for another four years.

Yet another task group was formed to prepare a church-wide study, collate congregational responses and prepare a report for the 1988 General Council in Victoria. Craig was asked to join the task group, along with 12 others representing the full spectrum of opinion within the United Church. By the time the task group released its report, "Towards a Christian Understanding of Sexual Orientations, Lifestyles and Ministry," in preparation for General Council there were petitions flooding in from all across the church. There had been non-stop media coverage, most of it tending to pick up the loudest and most polarized voices in the debate. The church had not experienced such a crisis since the decision to ordain women in 1936. That had taken 10 years of rancorous study and debate; some people had threatened to leave the church if women were ordained. And some did.

At General Council meetings sub-groups known as sessional committees sift through the material received and make recommendations to the larger body. Helen Hanna, a lay commissioner to the 1988 General Council from Montreal Presbytery, was assigned to Sessional Committee Eight, the one dealing with The Issue. When she left for General Council, Hanna wasn't quite sure how she felt about the issue of homosexuality and ministry, and she was more than a little apprehensive. "For me it was one of the most daunting tasks I've ever faced," she said, "but the actual sessional committee experience was one of the most wonderful ones I've ever had." It wasn't because committee members were all in agreement; quite the contrary. The group represented the full range of opinion that existed in the United Church at the time. Some on the committee were members of the Community of Concern and the United Church Renewal Fellowship, two United Church groups strongly opposed to gay and lesbian ordination. Hanna really valued their presence. "It was good to get to know them, and to appreciate their humanity," she said. "It forged some closer links."

Two gay and lesbian resource people were named to Sessional Committee Eight. For one of them, Allison Rennie, this experience continues to be a deeply significant moment in her spiritual life. "It's very much a pivotal point in terms of my commitment to the institution as separate from my faith," she says now. "It continues to stand as one of the most significant faith experiences and experiences of church and community I've ever had. What was riding on the decision of the General Council for me was basically staying in the church or not, because I had concluded that I had to work toward living as an out lesbian, and if I had to choose between doing that or being in the church, the church would lose. I had great despair that I would find a spiritual home anywhere else. The decisions that were made were significant affirmations that it was safe and wise and there was some integrity in my commitment to this institution."

The sessional committee struggled to find the best compromise it could amidst such a range of opinion and experience. Members agreed that they would work to consensus in their decisions. Instead of taking votes in which the majority "won" they tried to reach decisions with which everyone could live. "We worked through everything," said Hanna. This included mountains of petitions and letters. Because there was so much to deal with, members received material to read three months before General Council and began working together as a committee several days before the rest of the General Council commissioners arrived.

The sessional committee was chaired by Marion Best, a lay woman from British Columbia who later became Moderator from 1994 to 1997. Under her leadership, sessional committee members began by getting to know one another and building community across the lines that divided them. Hanna recalls some initial frustration with the amount of time this took. Later, realizing the impact it had, she is deeply appreciative. The strong sense of trust that emerged allowed committee members to speak freely and to respect one another. Even when their work went long into the night and nerves jangled, the respect remained.

One morning, the committee reconvened to find vicious and demeaning graffiti scrawled across the chalkboards of its classroom meeting space. With the graffiti there to speak for itself of the hatred that existed against gays and lesbians, committee members took a few moments of silence. Then they said the Lord's Prayer together before continuing with their morning's work.

Sessional Committee Eight reported twice to the General Council as a whole. The first time was a chance to test the water, to present some of its interim recommendations and receive feedback from the other commissioners. At 2:00 a.m. of the day they were to present for the first time, sessional committee members finally identified the basic points upon which they could agree. They were in accord with the church's previous statements on marriage. They recognized that the United Church had participated in injustice and discrimination against homosexuals and that there was a need for human rights legislation. And they were in agreement that the church had to discuss the issue of eligibility for *membership* before it talked about the criteria for accepting people into ordered ministry.

Marion Best presented the first report to the whole assembly, before asking for comment and feedback. She pointed out the very strong statements that the church had already made about marriage, family and sexuality. Some people seem to think the United Church "has no policies at all, as if we were proposing an 'anything goes' kind of morality," Best said. But that didn't stop some rather outrageous comments in the debate that followed.

The Rev. Morley Clarke, a commissioner from London, Ontario, wondered what might follow if the United Church approved of homosexuality—bestiality, necrophilia? He said that AIDS proved that homosexuals were unfit to be ministers. With barely controlled rage, the Rev. Brian Thorpe stepped to the microphone to disagree with what he later called "one of the most offensive things I've ever heard." Other commissioners lined up at the microphones to make their opinions heard, pro and con, and to suggest questions or compromises the sessional committee might consider.

Later in the evening, Anne Squire completed her term as United Church Moderator. Most people agree it was the stormiest and most turbulent two years ever faced by the United Church's highest elected officer. Commissioners had elected the Rev. Sang Chul Lee of Toronto as their next moderator. A soft-spoken and gentle man who grew up as a Korean refugee, Lee confessed that he had come to the General Council with very mixed opinions about homosexuality. He also admitted that he was somewhat scared of what he was getting himself into. "You should be," Squire called out.

In her closing remarks to the Council, Squire reminded commissioners of the key issue at the heart of this debate. "The question is whether we in the church can accept the ministry of gays and lesbians or whether we can tolerate erecting barriers to ministry ... and whether we plan to change The Basis of Union to place limitations on those whom Christ may call," she said. As she saw it, the debate, at its root, was about "whether we as a church will be an inclusive or exclusive body."

With a sheaf of written responses and the feedback from the floor, members of Sessional Committee Eight returned to their meeting room to continue their work. Somewhere along the line, the sessional committee decided to shelve the report "Toward a Christian Understanding of Sexual Orientations, Lifestyles and Ministry." The report had come to this General Council with the blessing of two of its Divisions, but it had provoked so much dissension across the church that it was time to start over. Committee members began to draft an entirely new report, "Membership, Ministry and Human Sexuality." At three in the morning, after a gruelling day, they went around the circle one last time and concluded that they had a statement on which, at least within the sessional committee, there was consensus. "We were all feeling pretty good about our decision at the end of the day," said Hanna. "I was disappointed that two people later backed away from what I thought had been a consensus." It wasn't perfect, but it was the best they could do. It was time to see what the rest of the General Council thought.

Step by step, inch by inch, the General Council worked through each of the recommendations. Speakers held up coloured cards to indicate whether they were speaking for or against a motion, or raising procedural questions. There were numerous attempts to amend or change the content. One motion—to define sexual orientation in such a way as to exclude sexual activity for all but married heterosexuals—was defeated.

Sessional Committee Eight presented a recommendation that existing processes for accepting people as members into the United Church should apply, and that all members could be considered to be ordained. An attempt to separate this into two separate motions—which would allow gays and lesbians as members but not ministers—also was defeated. There was another motion, to add a line to the statement saying God wanted fidelity in marriage and chastity and sexual abstinence for everyone else. Then there was an attempt to remove the reference to injustice against gays and lesbians or an acknowledgement of the gifts they offered to the church. Each time, commissioners considered the changes, and defeated them. There were a few minor amendments to the initial confessional statement of the report, and then it passed. But the bigger issue—the issue of homosexuality and ministry—was yet to be decided.

It was at this point in the proceedings that Sang Chul Lee stepped out of the chair. Citing his inexperience and fear that he might make procedural errors, he asked another former moderator, the Very Rev. Clarke MacDonald, to take over. MacDonald was someone well known for his commitment to issues of global justice, but had been outspoken in his opposition to the recommendations of the report "Toward a Christian Understanding of Sexual Orientations, Lifestyles and Ministry." With MacDonald in the chair, the final part of the report was before the Council: "That all persons, regardless of their sexual orientation, who profess Jesus Christ and obedience to Him, are welcome to be or become full members of the Church. All members of the Church are eligible to be considered for ordered ministry." The Council had already agreed that these two statements would stay together.

Next came a move to remove the words "regardless of sexual orientation." This would have left the statement saying absolutely nothing about the issue that had been before the church for so many years. There was more last-minute lobbying to have this phrase changed or removed. A motion to take an immediate vote passed. A motion to adjourn failed. Then came the vote on removing the phrase. The words "regardless of sexual orientation" stayed in. At 2:25 a.m., General Council adjourned for the night.

The next day, General Council took the final step—a vote on the entire statement, as amended. MacDonald, in spite of his reservations about sexual orientation and ministry, had earlier told the court that this statement was one with which he was willing to live. "I believe that what we have before us is the nearest we can come to honouring statements of the past, to honouring the appeals and petitions of the church, and to honouring the rights of persons regardless of their sexual orientation," he said. His words summed up the tension and difficulty this decision represented for the church. As someone who was highly respected by many on both sides of the debate, MacDonald's words carried weight. If he could live with this somewhat uneasy and imperfect compromise, perhaps they could, too.

When the final vote came it was, as usual, by show of hands. There was no official count, but those who were present say that somewhere between two thirds and three quarters of the commissioners voted in favour. Seventy-one commissioners requested that their dissenting vote be recorded. For better or worse, the debate was over. For now.

Everyone who was at the 1988 General Council has a story to tell. "I remember sitting weeping profusely when the final vote was taken," says one lesbian minister who sat in the visitors gallery throughout the debate. "It was partly relief, and yet it wasn't enough," she says. "The number of closeted gays and lesbians who were giving incredible up-front leadership at that General Council—how trashed they had been. The church will take the best gifts of these people and then trash them."

Gale Glover, now Alberta and Northwest Conference personnel minister, describes the moment as being "like the second chapter of Acts." That is the chapter that describes the early church's experience of Pentecost—the coming of the Holy Spirit with tongues of fire and rushing wind. "I was overwhelmed," Glover says. "It affirmed for me so much that we as a church were on the right path. The Spirit was really present with us as we were going through that struggle."

In August 1988, the 32nd General Council of The United Church of Canada made what many thought of as an historic decision. The irony is that it was in many ways a non-decision. The Council in essence voted not to change existing policy, that is, not to erect a barrier that had not existed previously. "All persons, regardless of their sexual orientation, who profess Jesus Christ and obedience to Him, are welcome to be or become full members of the Church," said the final statement. Nothing had changed. It has been the policy of the United Church since church union in 1925 not to exclude any group from membership. What the 1988 General Council did was to decide not to impose any new barriers. As for ordination, the question that was at the heart of this whole debate, the final resolution stated that "All members of the Church are eligible to be considered for ordered ministry." Again, nothing changed. That had been policy since the United Church came into being. All existing procedures for discerning and approving candidates for ministry were reaffirmed, from the congregation's role in putting forward candidates to the role of Conference in final recommendation for ordination and commissioning. Nothing changed. Everything changed.

For some people, the 1988 decision was a sign that the church had lost its spiritual centre. The Rev. Graham Scott described the General Council experience as "good people turning their backs on God." Many people wondered aloud if the United Church had thrown out the Bible along with all other traditional Christian teaching.

In fact, the United Church's struggles with the Bible were just beginning.

2

BODY AND SOUL

Faced with the choice between changing one's mind and proving there is no need to do so, almost everyone gets busy on the proof.

John Kenneth Galbraith

Christianity gave Eros poison to drink. She did not die of it, to be sure, but she degenerated into vice.

Friedrich Nietzsche

A small circle of worshippers is gathered around a lighted candle. They are singing a hymn. The tune is *Lauda Anima*. Most United Church people know it as "Praise, my soul, the king of heaven," but that's not the version this group is singing. The new words were written by the Rev. Sylvia Dunstan, a United Church minister. They reflect her commitment, while she was alive, to a spirituality in which bodies as well as souls are holy. It's a hymn sung often by gay and lesbian Christians.

> *Word made flesh! We see Christ Jesus*
> *Sharing our humanity.*
> *Loving, graceful, always truthful,*
> *Close to others bodily,*
> *Full of passion, full of healing,*
> *Touch of God to set them free.*
>
> *Wonderful are these our bodies,*
> *Flesh and blood to touch and see,*

Place of pain and contradiction,
Yet of joy and ecstasy,
Place of passion, place of healing,
Touched by God who sets us free.

One woman in the group is crying, and someone else reaches out an arm to encircle her. The hymn continues, building in volume.

O how glorious and resplendent,
Fragile body you shall be,
When endued with so much beauty,
Full of life and strong and free,
Full of vigour, full of pleasure,
That shall last eternally.

Glory give to God the Lover,
Grateful hearts to the Beloved,
Blessed be the love between them,
Overflowing to our good;
Praise and worship, praise and worship,
To the God whose name is love.

As the group sits down, someone reaches for the Kleenex box. The woman wipes away her tears. "I still can't sing that without crying," she says. "It's just that I've lived so many years as though I didn't have a body." She speaks of learning to live as a "head walking around without a body," as she tried to suppress and hide her emerging sexuality—that part of herself that she knew the world would abhor. She shut off part of herself in the process, the part that felt physical pleasure, comfort, passion. She denied herself the possibility of ever feeling whole in body and soul. Others in the group nod. They know what she means.

Most people grew up with explicit or veiled references from their Christian tradition that said that body was bad, body was "fallen," sinful, a source of dangerous and soul-destroying passions. They heard the story of the Garden of Eden interpreted with sexual overtones; the "fall" equated with sex. They remember that passage from Paul's first letter to the Corinthians: "For it is better to marry than to be aflame with passion." (1 Corinthians 7:9b) Some translations say "than to burn." Whatever Paul may have meant, many people mentally complete the phrase: "Better to marry than to burn in hell." For people who are married, or know that's an option in their lives—people who are heterosexual—these passages may not carry much emotional weight. But many gay and lesbian people hear them as total condemnation. For if heterosexuality is viewed by Christianity as some sort of evil, best contained by marriage, how much greater an evil is homosexuality.

Joan Hibbard knew she was "different" by the time she was in her late twenties. She had already fallen in love with more than one woman, and while these attractions felt as natural to her as the feelings her female friends had for their boyfriends, Hibbard lived with a well-defined set of religious beliefs. When in doubt, she turned to the Bible for guidance. But there, finding no positive biblical references to homosexuality, and a handful of very negative passages on homosexual behaviour, she felt confused and condemned. Hibbard read, she sought counselling, she prayed, and she wept. "I wept for all the tenderness, joy and passion, for the presence of God within me that I felt I would never be able to share in a loving, committed relationship," she writes. "I knew I would never love a man in that way. I wept for all the pain, the betrayal of myself that I carried around inside. I knew that I could not share it with others for fear of being labelled homosexual, or worse, a pervert." She developed a split, a dichotomy, between the part of herself known to her family and church and her "real self." She learned to hide, and to avoid certain questions—ones about romantic attachments to men, and about marriage.

"Mike" is still not ready to use his real name, but he does have a lot to say about issues of spirituality and sexuality. He describes it this way: "If you have learned all your life that it's impossible to be a healthy, whole person of faith and be gay, if you have been taught that what you feel in your body makes you worthless, perverted, evil, then it makes sense that you're going to separate your sense of the spiritual from your body." One way or another, you separate your body and your soul. Sometimes people do it by pretending they don't have a body. Others act as though they don't have a soul. Or, if they do, that it has no connection to their body. Mike describes the disembodied sexuality, all body but no soul, that he has encountered in some gay settings—where the only thing that counts is appearance, where relationships are reduced to brief encounters with anonymous strangers. Ironically, it has sometimes been the church that has led people to feel this is the only option for them to express their sexuality.

The Rev. Warren Eling lived most of his life quietly and unobtrusively as an Anglican priest, first in Toronto and later in Montreal. His death in December 1993 sent shock waves through the church. The Montreal parish where he served as priest was devastated. Initially the police said his death had nothing to do with his sexual orientation. It was just some crazy guy, a robber-murderer, robbing a priest. His first lover, however, declared publicly that the church was responsible for his murder, that the church had killed him with its homophobia. It had locked him in a closet, refused him safe relationships, and pushed him into a dangerous lifestyle of depersonalized sex.

It was certainly the church that prompted Eling to leave Toronto, in some haste, when another respectable priest was outed then immediately fired. So he fled to Montreal, which is where he died. Eling was well known to many gay United Church people in Montreal. The clergy sought one another out for mutual support. Friends said he knew he could never be in a "real" relationship, so he sought comfort instead with gay prostitutes and one-night stands. When the story finally unfolded, a gay prostitute was charged, and later convicted. The parish that had known him only as a respectable, nice, "single" priest was stunned.

At his funeral, the Anglican Bishop of Montreal publicly acknowledged the role that homophobia had played in Eling's death. By denying the possibility of a safe, healthy and whole relationship, the church had forced his sexuality underground, into a world where the body is just another expendable commodity. The church was an accomplice in Eling's death, said the Bishop.

Over the centuries, Christianity has become known as a religion that detests sexuality, the body and homosexuality most of all. Conservative Christians such as American singer and actress Anita Bryant, with her much-publicized campaign against homosexuality, and right-wing Christian protesters who show up at Gay Pride marches have given it a bad reputation.

Many gays and lesbians remember a Gay Pride march in Ottawa in the summer of 1996. Allan Sharpe, a member of Christ Baptist Fellowship Church, regularly carried a sign in the parade that stated, "The Bible says, neither fornicators nor idolaters, nor homosexuals nor sodomites will inherit the kingdom of God." Sharpe had been charged earlier in the year in connection with the destruction of hundreds of copies of *Capital Xtra*, an Ottawa gay/lesbian newspaper, at Hartman's Grocery Store. Sharpe was fined $500 and the judge ordered him to stay away from Hartman's and the offices of *Capital Xtra*. Other right-wing religious protesters also regularly carried signs that declared "AIDS is a queer disease" and "What's gay about a pervert?"

Ottawa resident John Morin decided to challenge homophobic religious protesters at the 1996 Pride march. With a sign that read "Jesus says love your neighbour as yourself," he stayed close beside Sharpe throughout the parade. Another person also marched close beside the religious right-wing protesters, wrapped in a rainbow flag and carrying a sign bearing the words "Jesus, protect me from your followers." Several women also decided to shadow, and challenge, right wing voices by carrying accepting and positive Bible verses. One of the women, Gillian Smith, said of her actions, "I want the world to get the message that there are Christians who believe in loving and accepting all human beings for what they are, and what God made them to be ... Jesus was not ever in favour of hurting people. He was in favour of love and support." One woman in a wheelchair travelled the parade route with a placard that announced "Celebrating sexual diversity, a gift from God!!"

It's because of all the negative messages about Christianity that some United Church people have taken to attending Gay Pride Day marches, with buttons and banners that proclaim loud and clear "The United Church of Canada Supports Gay and Lesbian People!"

"It's so important that people hear that message as well," says "Alex," a regular participant in Pride Day events, as well as a United Church member. "It is a reminder that Jesus didn't condemn people even though the rest of their culture did. He preached a message of love and acceptance." Alex thinks it's vital for gay people to discover that God doesn't condemn them either, that they can be both gay and spiritual.

Although Christianity has tended to disembody spirituality and love, there are many biblical passages that are extremely sensual and bodily.

As an apple tree among the trees of the wood,
so is my beloved among young men.
With great delight I sat in his shadow
and his fruit was sweet to my taste.
Song of Solomon 2:3

Oh, may your breasts be like clusters of the vine,
and the scent of your breath like apples
and your kisses like the best wine
that goes down smoothly,
gliding over lips and teeth.
Song of Solomon 7:8-9

These passages don't often get read in church on Sunday mornings, but they are there—reminders that our religious roots haven't always denied an embodied spirituality. Song of Solomon glorifies heterosexual passion, but there are also biblical stories of same-gender love. There is nothing in the story of David and Jonathan to indicate whether they were lovers or friends, but there is incredible passion, intensity and physicality in their relationship. David and Jonathan kiss, weep and embrace. "Your love to me was wonderful, passing the love of women," (2 Samuel 1:26b) proclaims David, upon hearing of Jonathan's death. In an earlier passage the biblical narrator tells us, "They kissed one another and wept with one another; David wept the more." (1 Samuel 20:41)

Gay and lesbian Christians have begun to discover biblical and spiritual affirmations of their bodily selves. We experience God's love in and through our bodies, in the sensual beauty and wonder of the created world, in our embodied emotions, and in the loving connection we have with others, including our lovers. Through our bodies we also live out our response. "God's steadfast love is not disembodied. It is found in the ground that anchors our feet, in the food that nourishes us through the day, in the arms that embrace us at night," writes gay theologian Chris Glaser in *The Word is Out*. "Nor is our faithfulness disembodied, but it is expressed in how we direct our feet, in how we transform the food to action, in how we embrace each other."

Colette Bazinet is a francophone who has lived all her life in Quebec. Although she was raised a Catholic, she became Protestant in 1978, when she joined the francophone congregation of Église St. Jean United Church in Montreal. She says she was looking for a church that was "not too right wing." The fact that the Moderator was a woman also indicated to her that this was a church where women had a significant role. The 1988 decision on sexual orientation and ministry confirmed Bazinet's decision. "The major impact was to give me one more reason to stay in the United Church," she says. "A mainstream church that can say that gays and lesbians can become ordained, it's a big step; it nourishes hope." She believes that Christianity is fundamentally a religion of incarnation. The word "incarnation" comes from a Latin word meaning "body" or "flesh." God is made known in physical, bodily form. "We live in our bodies, God is incarnate in us throughout the world," Bazinet says. "So the body is not some insignificant thing." Bazinet is lesbian and Christian. She has found a spiritual home in a church she believes affirms all of who she is.

Joan Hibbard also found peace in her own journey of accepting that she could be both lesbian and a faithful Christian. The struggle between the reality of her personhood and the belief that any expression of homosexuality was sinful continued for several years. She believes, however, that God has worked through people, experiences and the in-dwelling presence of God's Spirit to bring a healing and integration in her life that she never thought possible. Affirm, an organization of United Church gays, lesbians and bisexuals, was an important source of support. "I have come to love myself as a sexual being—as a physical and spiritual being," she says. "I have come to value my sexual orientation as a gift from God, a gift that can be expressed in loving, committed relationship. To be other than what I know myself to be would be like a crocus fussing and striving to be a tulip because the world valued tulips more!" Not all United Church people see it that way.

In a 1960 statement, the United Church declared that homosexuality was a sin. Homosexuality was a sin, said the statement, because it violated God's will for "proper" sexual expression within monogamous marriage. It was a sin because it misused "natural functions." It was a sin because it involved other partners and was therefore "unedifying and destructive of neighbour love." And it was a sin because it undermined "the foundations of a stable society based on heterosexual marriage and family responsibility."

In 1988, the United Church confessed a very different sin—a sin in which the whole church had participated through its "history of injustice and persecution against gay and lesbian persons, in violation of the Gospel of Jesus Christ."

The Bible was an essential underpinning of both statements. The Bible is, after all, central to the life of the United Church. The Basis of Union of the United Church declares that Holy Scriptures are the "primary source and ultimate standard of Christian faith and life." The United Church didn't change its mind on that point in 1988. It continued to assert that "God speaks authoritatively" through the Bible.

Two statements, 28 years apart, both claiming to take the Bible seriously, came to radically different conclusions. No wonder the United Church decided in 1988 that it needed a church-wide study on the authority and interpretation of scripture. No wonder some people began to question what the Bible *really* says about homosexuality.

In fact, the Bible doesn't say very much about homosexuality, not as much as some people suppose. There is no word specifically for "homosexuality" anywhere in the Bible because the concept of homosexuality as a sexual orientation only originated in the nineteenth century. There are a few biblical references to homosexual behaviour and some other passages that in later years have been used to condemn homosexuals. One of the most oft-cited Bible stories—the story of Sodom and Gomorrah in Genesis 19:1-11—turns out not to be about homosexuality at all. This, even though from post-biblical times to the present the word "sodomite" has become almost synonymous with homosexuality.

In the story two angels encounter Abraham's nephew, Lot, at the city gate in Sodom. Lot offers them hospitality at his house. Perhaps thinking the strangers are spies, the men of Sodom surround Lot's house and demand that Lot "bring them out to us so that we may know them." The word "know" (in Hebrew *yad ha'*) is used a few times in Hebrew scripture to mean "to have sexual intercourse with" so translators have sometimes assumed that is what it means here. Scholars, however, point out that *yad ha'* is only used to denote heterosexual intercourse. For homosexual intercourse the word *shakhabh* is used consistently.

Lot attempts to placate the men of Sodom by offering them his two virgin daughters, begging them not to harm his guests because that would violate his obligation to offer hospitality to strangers. The story concludes when the two angels strike all the men of Sodom with blindness. Many scholars think the story is about violating laws of hospitality of the time, which decreed that a guest in one's house was inviolable. As biblical scholar John Boswell points out, hospitality laws were enforced by threat of death by God because in those times travel would have been dangerous and often fatal were it not for people taking travellers in for the night.

Indeed, when the prophets (Isaiah 1:10-17, Jeremiah 23:14, Ezekiel 16:49-50) and Jesus (Luke 10:10-12) referred to Sodom and Gomorrah, they talked not about homosexuality or even homosexual acts but about immorality in general—gluttony, social injustice, not offering welcome to strangers, not caring for the poor.

There are two passages in the Hebrew scriptures that specifically condemn homosexual acts. In the holiness code of Leviticus, under penalty of death, a man is prohibited from "lying with a man as with a woman." (Leviticus 18:22 and 20:13) It is important to note, in looking at these verses in their original context, that they are part of a much larger list of rules and regulations. Some United Church people are quick to cite these verses, at the same time ignoring rules against eating shrimp, rabbit, and pork (Leviticus 11); against cross-breeding animals, planting two kinds of seed in the same field or wearing clothing made of two different kinds of material (Leviticus 19:19); against tattoos and certain kinds of haircuts (Leviticus 19:27-28); or any of countless other ritual obligations not observed in The United Church of Canada.

Many of the obligations of the Holiness Code in Leviticus are designed to distinguish early Israelite society from that of its pagan neighbours. They are rules about separation (hence the importance of avoiding "mixtures") and about separateness. Some scholars say that the sexual prohibitions in Leviticus against homosexual behaviour have less to do with homosexuality and more to do with distinguishing Israelite society from certain ritualized sexual acts in the religious observances of its Canaanite neighbours. "Do not defile yourselves in any of these ways, for by all of these practices the nations I am casting out (of the land of Canaan) have defiled themselves," reads Leviticus 18:24, after a list of prohibitions that includes handing over one's children to be used in the worship of the god Molech.

There are no references to homosexuality or homosexual acts in the Gospels and only a very few references in the Epistles. One of Paul's letters has a list of people who will not inherit the kingdom of God (1Corinthians 6:9-10) Along with drunkards, robbers and thieves, Paul lists fornicators, adulterers and *arsenokoitai*, a Hebrew word variously translated as "sodomites" or "homosexual perverts" that literally means "men who are sexually promiscuous with men." A similar list of vices appears in another epistle (1 Timothy 1:10). The most extensive condemnation of homosexual acts occurs in Paul's letter to the church in Rome:

> *For this reason God gave them up to degrading passions. Their*
> *women exchanged natural intercourse for unnatural, and in the*
> *same way also the men, giving up natural intercourse with women,*
> *were consumed with passion for one another. Men committed shame-*
> *less acts with men and received in their own persons the due penalty*
> *for their error.*
> Romans 1:26-32

The passage is unambiguous in its condemnation of homosexual acts, which Paul believed were unnatural, and therefore against God's law. Paul was a Jew, trained in the Law and observant of the Holiness Code. Furthermore, Paul had no notion of the concept of homosexuality as an orientation that might make same-gender love quite natural for a certain percentage of the population.

❦

Ken DeLisle is now a United Church minister, but he was raised in a conservative Catholic family, a family that took the Bible seriously. Not surprisingly, when he first started to realize he might be gay he believed it was a sin, it was wrong and he had to change. DeLisle continued to deny that he was gay throughout high school and university, and later determined to change his sexual orientation. He sought therapy that included treatment with electric shocks. After three years of behaviour modification he was pronounced "cured" of all homosexual tendencies. Six months later the feelings resurfaced. DeLisle signed up for another round of shock treatments. But he never made it to the session. He went to a gay men's group instead. "I had this vision of being married and saying to my wife, 'not tonight dear, I haven't had my shock treatments,'" he says. "I'm not fighting who I am any longer. God must have a mission for me. I'm going to tell the whole world that homosexuality is not a curse, it's a gift."

Gradually, DeLisle was able to move beyond a literal interpretation of those passages of scripture and hear other messages in the Bible, messages that spoke of personal integrity, of being made in God's image, of being the person God calls you to be. He remembers a turning point in his life when he heard the story of the prophet Elijah read in church. God was calling Elijah to come out of a cave where he was hiding. Elijah protested, "But they're killing all of us." Elijah eventually came out of his cave, and so did DeLisle. "When I came out of the closet and accepted myself as a gay person I determined to do whatever I could so that other people wouldn't have to go through the pain and tragedy I went through," he says. He went on to study theology and became the first openly gay candidate for diaconal ministry in the United Church. He was commissioned on May 29, 1994, by Manitoba and Northwestern Ontario Conference.

DeLisle went through a transformation in his view of scripture, from looking only at the passages that condemn homosexuality to hearing in the Bible messages of hope and self-acceptance, even for gay people. There isn't anything very new in that. Even though some people claim that the church is picking and choosing which scriptures to follow and which to ignore, in fact that is exactly what all United Church people do, even the most conservative ones. Even when dealing with Paul and the other epistles, the Chris-

tian church has made decisions contrary to the prescriptions of these letters, allowing women to speak and have their heads uncovered in church,
for example, (1 Corinthians 11:6,10) and rejecting slavery as an institution
ordained by God (1 Timothy 61-2).

❧

Église St. Jean United Church blends unobtrusively into its surroundings,
an aging stone building in the heart of Montreal's red-light district. A prostitute lurches out from the corner to hail a truck stopped at the light. The
truck moves on. "All I need is five more bucks so I can get off my feet and
get home," she mutters, to no one in particular. A few blocks further down
the street, past the sex shops, video stores and strip joints is "the village"—
the gay district. Here are bars and clubs catering to a different clientele.
Teenagers hang out all along the strip, many of them prostitutes and addicts. A few joints, a few beer bottles. And a church. One is reminded of the
small minority churches that the Apostle Paul wrote to, churches struggling
to survive, to be a voice of conscience and morality in the vice-ridden cities
of the Greek and Roman world.

The Rev. Denis Fortin is minister here, in an aging congregation whose
neighbourhood has changed. "If we wanted to judge the heterosexual world
[on the basis of] the examples we've got around here, it would really be a
caricature," he says. "It's consumerism oriented to a certain segment of the
population. The problem for some parishioners is that they identify homosexual living with the 'village' stereotypes in a way that they don't identify
heterosexual lifestyle with the red-light district."

There's lots of nostalgia for the good old days at Église St. Jean, and a lot
of talk about the Bible. Fortin doesn't believe the church is stuck with a
literal interpretation of scripture, not on women, slavery, a flat earth, or
homosexuality. The Gospels are silent on the subject of homosexuality. But
they are not silent on justice, compassion, love of neighbour. It's those passages that Fortin looks to, scriptures that speak of the "all-encompassing
love of God." At first reading it does look as though the Bible rules out
homosexuality, he explains, but you have to look at the larger picture. Those
same epistles that tell women to be silent in church and slaves to return to
their masters also talk of oneness in Christ that transcends human catego-
ries—male and female, slave and free, Jew or Greek. Perhaps even gay and
straight.

Fortin thinks it was no coincidence that the church undertook to review its understanding of scripture at the same time as the ordination de-

bate, because "if you're literal in your interpretation, you're stuck with a condemnation of homosexuality."

❦

The Rev. Loraine MacKenzie Shepherd has been ministering in United Church congregations since 1986. Ordained in 1991, she is currently doing doctoral studies at Emmanuel College in Toronto. MacKenzie Shepherd was in a three-point charge in rural Saskatchewan when The Issue hit. She recalls those years in the life of the United Church as a horrendous time. One of the points where she served passed a motion saying it would never hire a homosexual minister. The two other points said they didn't feel comfortable excluding anyone so the motion was defeated by the official board. A couple of people left. MacKenzie Shepherd recalls pastoral visits with people who were furious with the United Church's decision. She went, trying to douse the flames. "Regardless of your sexual orientation, it was a horrendous time for any minister," she notes. "There were some very vocal people, some horrid stuff." She doesn't elaborate.

As part of her doctoral work, MacKenzie Shepherd did extensive study of the 1988 United Church decision in contrast to the 1960 statement that declared homosexuality a sin. How did the United Church use the Bible in 1988 and was it different from the way the church interpreted scripture in the past?

In its 1988 decision, some people felt that the United Church had abandoned its traditional moral standards and ways of interpreting the Bible. MacKenzie Shepherd concluded that the United Church has always taken culture and science seriously in its theological and ethical deliberations. In coming to the conclusions that it did, the church didn't just succumb to culture and ignore tradition and the Bible. She found that, in 1960, just as in 1988, the reports seriously considered biblical and traditional sources and were critical of particular social trends. At the same time, "true to United Church and reform tradition, [they] reject biblical literalism and seek to interpret the scripture holistically and contextually, in the spirit of Christ," she says. She found a remarkable consistency, across several decades, in the church's approach to scripture. It didn't pull out particular passages as proof texts, but always attempted to look at the whole of scripture in light of the message of Jesus Christ. All the documents, she says, "were adamantly opposed to literalist and legalistic interpretations. All stressed that scripture be read within the context of the entire Bible and understood within Jesus' command to love God and neighbour as oneself.

Passages that seemed at odds with Jesus' compassionate approach were dismissed as culturally specific."

Basically, the United Church said, and has always said, that scripture must be interpreted in light of the overall message of Jesus, in light of Christian tradition, in light of our own experience and in light of our culture. In 1960, as in 1988, the United Church used very similar methods and approaches in its interpretation. How, then, did it come to such very different conclusions? What changed was our experience, our understanding of social sciences and our culture. Through the '70s and '80s there was an increasing acceptance of gay and lesbian people. Legislation also changed. In 1969 then-Prime Minister Pierre Trudeau ordered the state out of the "bedrooms of the nation" and civil codes decriminalized homosexuality. Psychology and psychiatry no longer considered homosexuality to be a mental disorder. The church was confronted with an understanding of homosexuality as a difference, like right or left handedness, not a deviance. And, perhaps most significantly of all, it was offered face-to-face encounters, as gays and lesbians came out in their workplace, families, even their churches.

The Rev. Peter Wyatt now works as a general secretary in the United Church, with responsibility for a portfolio called "theology, faith and ecumenism." He exemplifies the change of opinion for many in the United Church. He has always taken scripture very seriously as "the cradle of the living word of Jesus Christ," he says. He still does. He has always viewed it as authoritative for his life and faith. That, too, has remained unchanged. What *have* changed are his beliefs about homosexuality. In 1981 Wyatt was a minister in a congregation when a young man came to see him who had just experienced an evangelical conversion. He talked quite openly with Wyatt about his lack of attraction to the opposite sex and how that had plagued a number of his relationships. They talked, they opened the Bible. Wyatt suggested he would do well to seek some counselling because he didn't think all the answers were in the pages of the Bible.

In 1982, Wyatt was asked to write a theological reflection for a United Church issue paper called "Homosexuals and the Church in Dialogue." He looked at Paul's letters, and other scriptures, and concluded that "while defending the civil rights of homosexually oriented people, the Church must nonetheless make clear that homosexual practices are divinely forbidden."

A year or so later the gay man came back to see Peter to talk about the article. The young man described his experiences in what he called "the urban homosexual jungle." Then, with controlled anger in his voice, he said, "we don't need condemnation from the church. We've got enough self-condemnation, thank you very much. We need a little encouragement to live in responsible relationships."

Wyatt looks back on that moment as a turning point. He began to read. When he was elected a commissioner to the 1988 General Council he decided he'd better meet some more gay and lesbian people, because he didn't know what he was going to do when faced with decisions at Council. Through meeting and really listening to gay and lesbian people, Wyatt says he discovered, "that as normal and natural as heterosexual attraction was for me, so normal and natural it felt for them to be attracted to the same sex."

He notes that for most people who want to write same-sex love out of the civilized world, their real objection is not that it's anti-scriptural, but that it's unnatural. That's what gets them in the gut. The light went on for Wyatt when he met people who started to tell him that what's natural for him may not be natural for them. As for the Bible, he says, "I sorted it out in my own mind as much as I'll ever sort it out. There seems to be something called 'sexual orientation' that Paul didn't know about. Paul would have thought that any homosexual act was going against nature and therefore in defiance of the Creator of nature. The whole concept of homosexuality simply didn't exist in Paul's day."

Wyatt compares it to Galileo saying that we live in a heliocentric (sun-centred) solar system, not an earth-centred universe. "It feels like the foundations of scriptural authority are shaken and yet, somehow, we manage to accommodate ongoing scientific discovery with ongoing respect for what we believe is the essential word of God in the scripture."

Asked what he thinks now about the theological reflection he wrote in 1982, Wyatt chuckles: "It's been quite a journey! Thank goodness we have a few years to live and can sometimes allow ourselves to be educated by them."

3

PICKING UP THE PIECES

There is no squabbling so violent as that between people who accepted an idea yesterday and those who will accept the same idea tomorrow.

Christopher Morley

Alice Potts is another child of the United Church. She grew up in the church, and has served many years on presbytery in British Columbia, chairing her presbytery from 1977-79. She has attended two General Councils, and is currently involved with outreach and stewardship in the United Church Women (U.C.W.). She still finds that it hurts to recall the years leading up to 1988. "It's history now, and I hope we can continue to learn from the lessons of that terrible time," she says. Potts describes feeling increasingly disenfranchised in her home congregation: "I didn't dare voice an opinion that differed from what appeared to be the majority." It really wasn't a comfortable way to worship and participate.

At one point, Potts put a note in a local paper. "My husband and I are members of The United Church of Canada and fully support its decisions and doctrine. Are there any others who feel as we do?"

Shortly afterwards, she heard about a split that was looming at Comox United Church and gladly joined up to become part of the remnant congregation that chose to remain there. As she describes it, "the lonely United Church people began to surface." She recalls the wonderful feeling of finding, once again, a church home. It wasn't a place where everyone agreed; it was a place where all opinions could be respected. She points out that the even for those who remained at Comox United, response to The United Church of Canada's position was by no means unanimous. "When the expanded board discussed the statement, all we could agree on was the preamble, but when we left the meeting, we were all friends," she explains. This is the key for Potts: being able to differ, and yet still remain in loving community with one another.

ॐ

Marion Best works as an educator at Naramata Centre, a United Church lay education facility in Winfield, British Columbia. It's a peaceful setting, on the edge of a lake, in the middle of the Okanagan Valley. Best went back home to Naramata after the 1988 General Council, and there she was somewhat sheltered from the storm that swirled around the rest of the church. It was only after she became United Church Moderator in 1994 that she heard how hard things were for the other members of the sessional committee she chaired. "Since being Moderator I have met, with one or two exceptions, everyone who was on that sessional committee, and every one of them has a story to tell about what it was like when they went back home, how abusive and difficult it was in many places," she says. Best still has a lot of sadness about that, but she stands by the decision—a decision that, at the time, "felt quite a modest one," she says. "I still believe we did the best we could at that time, given where we were and who we were."

After all, the statement was a compromise. Many people who support gay and lesbian rights felt it didn't go nearly far enough. Best admits that in many parts of its final report, the church remained deliberately ambiguous. "The statement referred to 'life lived in obedience to Christ.' Who's going to define what that means?" she asks. That interpretation remained in the hands of local congregations. It was clear to her that the Council wanted a somewhat open-ended statement, one where there was still some room. No congregation was going to be forced to accept gay and lesbian people or clergy. "You can't legislate these things," she says. "To tell a congregation they have to accept someone—they'd just make life miserable for them until they left!"

That may have been what the official document said, but that's not what everyone heard. With headlines that proclaimed "United Church votes to ordain homosexuals," the media declared that the church had flung open the door to gay ordination. Opponents of the ordination of gays and lesbians said that congregations now would be forced to have homosexual clergy. The way the Rev. Sharon Moon sees it, those who were against the decision pushed it far further than the General Council had ever intended.

Moon, a minister at First United Church in Ottawa, was outspoken in her support for gay and lesbian rights before, and at, the 1988 General Council.

Initially she didn't get the impression that those who supported gay and lesbian concerns had gained a great deal. But those who disagreed with Council's decision saw it differently. "It's my perception that those who were opposed to the decision, those who wanted total exclusion of gays and lesbians, declared a victory for their opponents." The statement itself didn't change much, but it was interpreted as going much further. And it was the interpretation that sent shock waves across the church.

People did leave, though not nearly as many as some had predicted. Most mainline Canadian denominations are losing members at a similar rate, so it is hard to give an exact figure linked to the impact of the decision. But an analysis of membership trends over the years of The Issue suggests as many as 25,000 people may have left because of the General Council decision. This includes 70 ministry personnel (from a total of about 4,000) and significant portions of 60 congregations (out of approximately 4,100 preaching points). These numbers do not record the rebound effect, as people came back to United Churches they had previously left or as people from the community joined because they now felt they had a church home where they would be welcomed. Many congregations that lost significant portions of their membership speak of this as the time of "the split."

Marjorie Boulton is 92, and a member at First United Church, Lethbridge, Alberta. She is partially deaf and, as she puts it, not as active as she once was. She taught Sunday school for many years, and was a member of her church board when the split happened. That was on a fateful Sunday shortly after the 1988 General Council decision. Members were asked to vote on whether they wanted to remain with First United, and The United Church of Canada, or follow their dissident minister to form a new church.

Those who were leaving, 133 of them, walked out of the church building. Only 27 people remained in the pews. Boulton was one of them. "We felt we were right; we were United Church." She think that's what the split was really about: People talked about The Issue but really it was about what it meant to be The United Church of Canada.

Betty Chollock has been United Church all her life. She joined First United, Lethbridge, in 1951. She is a long-time member of the board, and chaired it in 1994. Chollock is what she calls "traditional" when it comes to being United Church. Of homosexuality she says, "It's not a lifestyle I would choose, but that's not a reason to judge or condemn." She figures that the 1988 decision left room for a wide range of opinions. "General Council left it open to the local church to do what was right for them. I don't think we would ever call an [openly] gay or lesbian minister. But the people who left couldn't accept any degree of openness."

The split at First United didn't happen overnight. There had been increasing tension and disagreement between members and their minister at the time, the Rev. Bill Calderwood. Many people, including Chollock, liked Calderwood personally, but disagreed with his fundamentalist theology and his charismatic worship style. "I couldn't agree with things he was preaching," says Chollock, "and some of the services..." her voice trails off. "There was lots of evangelical fervour, singing the same songs over and over; it was like a cult." Many people had drifted away long before the split. When the General Council issued its statement on sexual orientation, Calderwood preached a series of blistering sermons. The congregation's Mission and Service Fund contributions weren't sent in to the national church, says Chollock. For some, this was the final straw.

After the split, the congregation slowly began to pick up the pieces. Calderwood formed the First Congregational church in Lethbridge, and many see that as an ideal solution for everyone. People at First United Church still speak of him with respect. "I'm still good friends with Bill," explains Chollock, "we just disagree with each other's opinions." There seems to be both tolerance and a willingness to coexist peaceably. Chollock's grandson and wife attend First Congregational. Chollock recently went there for the baptism of her great-grandson. "It was a nice baptismal service," she says. But the rest of the service wasn't really her thing.

First United rebounded slowly. About 50 people who had drifted away when Calderwood was minister came back. Others from the community were attracted in by the dynamic ministry, a welcoming atmosphere, and strong concern for outreach. The congregation is now close to 300 families, with 30 children in the Sunday school. There are plans to start a youth group in the fall. Giving is up and finances are fine. Chollock is full of praise for the congregation and its current minister, the Rev. Yvonne Jordan. "We have gone out and tried to be welcoming of all people," she says. "The church is really growing."

As for The Issue, it isn't talked about much. "I don't think it's a problem," says Marjorie Boulton. Chollock doesn't know of any gay and lesbian people in the congregation, but, she adds, "a lot of people have changed their minds." She is one of them.

A little further north in Alberta is the Carmangay-Champion pastoral charge. It faced a much more serious problem when, in 1989, its minister led the majority of members and adherents out to form a Congregational church in the community. With income drastically reduced, the remaining members of the pastoral charge wondered how they could possibly continue.

Foothills Presbytery gave them much encouragement during this difficult time. The pastoral charge obtained a Mission and Service grant. They recruited ministers Bert and Ev Frey and later Frank and Shirley Johnson. At first, the charge encountered considerable hostility from the many people in the Champion community who had left the United Church. But the ministry was a healing one, and over the next five years some of the hurt and anger in the community diminished.

Despite a loyal membership of only 20 to 25 members, the charge organized fund-raising suppers, walk-a-thons, garage sales, and many other activities to maintain its Mission and Service objective of more than $4,800, close to 20 per cent of its total operating budget. In 1995, the pastoral charge amalgamated with nearby Vulcan, to form what is now the Westwinds Pastoral Charge. The Rev. Don and Brenda Watt work there as a ministry team.

"There is still incredible pain in the community," says Don. Just as things were beginning to settle, they got stirred up all over again when an evangelical crusade came to town, with the United Church as its target. The issues? Biblical literalism, inclusive language and, of course, the United Church's position on homosexuality. Friendships were lost. Some families were split right down the middle. Local businesses were told they would lose customers if they went to the United Church. Don doesn't think it was just about homosexuality. "It isn't The Issue that split the church. If that issue hadn't been there, it would have been other things," he says. "There are people who are simply not willing to be open and tolerant of other people even though they are different. Those are the people who split the church. The Issue was just a handy tool."

Brenda makes it a priority in her ministry to affirm people for who they are and the work they are doing as a United Church. One of the preaching points on the pastoral charge was down to a handful of people after the split. "Now they are paying their own way and contributing to the Mission and Service Fund," she says with obvious pride. But there is still pain. "People still cry when they talk about what happened."

"Jane" is a long-time member of the pastoral charge. She remembers when the evangelist came to town. "He said we weren't Christian," she recalls, "and that we didn't support the Bible." Jane's son and daughter-in-law left the United Church at that time to join a church that takes the Bible literally. That created a huge rift in the family. "My son pleaded with us to leave the United Church because he felt sure we were doomed," she says sadly.

The rift ran deep in the community, too. Jane recalls many occasions when the town used to work together ecumenically—at joint services for Remembrance Day, Good Friday, the town's anniversary, or the World Day of Prayer. "Then all of a sudden we were just ostracized. They won't take part if the United Church is involved." That's hard in a community where most people have very close ties. "We all grew up together. Most of us have lived here all our lives," she adds.

Jane personally agrees with the United Church's decision: "I'm fully supportive of gays and lesbians. A lot of people think of gays and lesbians as being perverted and they don't want anything to do with them. I wouldn't want a perverted homosexual in the pulpit, but of course I wouldn't want a perverted heterosexual in the pulpit either!" But that's not the main reason she has stayed in the United Church. Many of those who stayed disagree with the United Church's decision, but still see themselves as United Church. "There is still diversity in the United Church, and people who stayed don't all think the same way," she explains. "That is what attracts some people to the United Church: that we don't all have to think the same in order to be part of a loving congregation. We can agree and disagree and agree to disagree and carry on."

Westwinds Pastoral Charge is still struggling to survive and be that kind of Christian community, and is having a much harder time than others, such as First United in Lethbridge. Perhaps it is the size of the community—in a larger town such as Lethbridge there may be more options for people to live and let live with their differences in opinion. Relationships may be less intertwined. When small rural churches lose members, however, people know this may well be the death of their church and that added sense of vulnerability may make it harder to move on. In a small community there are also not many other people "out there" who may be willing to help rebuild a struggling church. Whatever the reasons, it seems that small churches in small communities faced the greatest obstacles when splits occurred.

In March 1988, several United Church ministers in the Comox-Nanaimo region of Vancouver Island put an ad in the local paper. Under the banner "Sexual Lifestyles?!" they rejected the essence of the United Church report "on the ordination of practising homosexual persons and the condoning of extramarital sexual relations." They warned that they were exploring "various alternatives, including the possibility of establishing a new association of congregations," should the recommendations be adopted as United Church policy. The same storm that had swept through other United Church congregations was brewing here as well.

Eleanor Martin was born in Vancouver in 1925, just after the United Church was founded. She grew up in a solidly United Church household, raised to believe that "one great strength of the United Church lay in the diversity of its membership. I grew up believing that there was a place for each of us in God's plan," she explains. Martin joined Comox United Church in 1948, and over the years taught Sunday school and led youth groups. In the years leading up to 1988, she watched the congregation change. "Before 1988, [it] had become increasingly rigid, with a right way and a wrong way. As a member of the second group, I frequently felt preached at."

Martin painfully recalls the events at a congregational meeting on October 5, 1988: "A large screen, which effectively obscured the cross, was raised, and on it was projected a list of the sins committed." Then a motion was made: "We do not accept the authority of The United Church of Canada and its courts. We declare our intention to dissociate from it..." Of the 122 votes cast, 99 were in favour. Twenty-two were opposed.

Rosemary Lyle had been a member of Comox United long before 1988. She recalls being approached by elders and asked how she felt about homosexuals giving leadership in the church. Because she wasn't comfortable with this, she agreed to attend a meeting to discuss the issue. She was somewhat appalled to discover that the October 5 meeting "was not a discussion but a pre-arranged plan ... to break away from The United Church of Canada." She found the meeting "autocratic and not democratic. Free discussion was denied." When the time came to vote, Lyle voted against leaving the church. Ultimately it had to do with very United Church beliefs about openness and inclusion. "I believe that any church should be open to whomever wishes to worship," she declares. "It really had less to do with the homosexual issue than with my sense of justice."

The small handful of people who remained part of Comox United Church divided up the tasks and responsibilities of being a church. Joan Boorman was one of the people who, as she puts it, "came out of the woodwork and back to church." Boorman and her husband had moved to Comox in 1981. Both are retired health professionals who had been a part of the United Church all their lives. Boorman had a hard time finding a church home in her new community. The local churches were what she describes as "quite fundamentalist." The Boormans were among many others who joined Comox United only after the split, and have been active there ever since. This influx of people from the community who would never have felt comfortable in that congregation under its previous leadership was a vital factor in rebuilding the congregation.

Margaret Palmeter agrees. She's another United Church stalwart and long-time member of Comox United. As Palmeter explains, those in the congregation who disagreed with The United Church of Canada's position "felt strongly that it was wrong but it [The United Church of Canada] was their church despite this." For others, homosexuality simply wasn't an issue. What helped the little group move on was what Boorman calls its compassionate spirit. "We agreed to respect where each of us was coming from and get on with rebuilding the Comox United Church family, and we did!" she concludes emphatically.

The small remnant worked together, socialized together, prayed together and watched the church grow. Leadership was important during that rebuilding time. The ministerial leadership of the Rev. Robert Stiven modelled warmth, compassion, openness to differences and respect. A small group of very dedicated lay people committed themselves to rebuilding a church, to what Palmeter calls "the nuts and bolts of survival as a congregation." Whatever other differences they had, the group was united on that score. Today, 10 years later, there are 229 households on the Comox United Church roll. There are now more than a hundred people on an average Sunday. In 1988, following the split, there were six children left in the congregation. Now there are more than 70. Children are visible, lay people are active, outreach programs are vibrant. The building is busy six days a week. Worship services are lively and diverse. As Martin describes it, "services range from serene and inspirational, to thought provoking and inspirational, to merrily muddled..." Here, she pauses, "and inspirational!" In all its diversity, Comox United Church is alive and well.

4

Public Vows

Genuine beginnings begin within us, even when they are brought to our attention by external opportunities.

William Bridges

Entreat me not to leave you,
Or to turn back from following after you:
For wherever you go, I will go;
And wherever you lodge, I will lodge;
Your people shall be my people,
And your God my God.
Ruth 1:16

Rachael is in four-year-old heaven as flower girl at her aunt's wedding. A frilly dress, brand new white shoes, flowers in her hair and daisy petals in her basket, socks with lace ruffles—what more could one ask for? She doesn't know her aunt very well, nor her aunt's partner, since they live some distance away. In spite of the careful preparation her parents tried to give her she is still a bit confused about the gender of these two who are to be married. Both are women. In an earlier discussion with her mother about the possibility of same-gender relationships, Rachael concluded emphatically "But Mom, when there's a princess there has to be a prince!" She spends most of the day of the wedding trying to figure out if her aunt's partner really is a woman. By the end of the day, though, she's convinced that she is. The ceremony proceeds, with two United Church family members presiding. It's just like any other wedding on a sunny Saturday in May, except for the gender. At bedtime that evening, a sleepy and totally contented little flower girl is helped out of her dress and into her pyjamas. As her mother places her flowers in water, Rachael takes a moment to arrange the wonderful fancy socks, with the ruffles standing up, in her new shoes. As she does so, she has a little private conversation with them, as though they are some imaginary wedding party. "You can be the girl," she says to one shoe. And then to the other, "And you can be the boy. No, no, you can both be girls. You can be Alison and you can be Theresa!"

❧

When the split occurred for the church in Lachine, Quebec, it happened a great many years ago. In 1925, to be exact. There are now two churches called St. Andrew's in Lachine. There used to be just one.

St. Andrew's Presbyterian was built in 1818 in a close-knit, working-class community. Lachine is now more or less a suburb of Montreal, but it still has strong family ties going back to its original Scottish roots. The small stone church building overlooking the lake was, and still is, an important community institution. In 1925, at the time of church union when The United Church of Canada came into being, most Presbyterians voted to join the new church. St. Andrew's Presbyterian became St. Andrew's United Church. However, across Canada there were some Presbyterians who didn't join in at union. They formed the Presbyterian Church in Canada. Some of those folk helped build a new Presbyterian church in Lachine. They called it St. Andrew's. Some would say it was an act of defiance, and there were strong feelings at the time as families and friends found themselves torn asunder.

Members of the two St. Andrew's churches share a common history. Most of them were born and raised in Lachine. They worked together in the steel plants. Their children grew up together. They retired together. Eventually these bonds proved stronger than the divisions that happened in 1925. The two St. Andrew's, one Presbyterian and one United, don't do much together ecumenically, but socially they're one community. Most people are members of the same 50+ club, which meets in the United Church. On Wednesdays, they all play cribbage at the Anglican Church. They all go to each other's church teas and strawberry socials.

There was no major split in 1988 at St. Andrew's United, perhaps because some could still remember the 1925 division, perhaps because they didn't want another big debacle. For whatever reason, the issue wasn't talked about, not publicly at any rate. There was no formal debate, no big meetings, no motions to pull out of the United Church. Most people probably opposed the General Council decision, but said nothing. Homosexuality wasn't discussed, not for another six years. And when it did come up, it was the Presbyterians down the street who started it.

Darryl Macdonald was born into a very close, loving and fairly strict Nova Scotian Presbyterian family. He recalls not being allowed to go to movies on Sunday. His early life revolved around the church—choirs, Sunday school, cubs, youth group. In the eighth grade, inspired by a generous and caring minister, he made up his mind that he, too, would become a Presbyterian minister. At that time, he simply took it for granted that gays were one of those groups condemned to hell. "That's what I was taught, that's what I believed, even before I knew what they were," he says. Even before he knew he was gay.

While in undergraduate studies, Macdonald came to terms with being gay. By the time he entered Presbyterian College, Montreal, to study theology, he was clear both about himself and his vocation. As he entered the college, he recalls thinking to himself, "this is where I'm going to learn good theology, and this is where I'm going to learn to be gay and Christian and Presbyterian." He graduated in 1989, but didn't immediately seek a call. (In the Presbyterian system, candidates must receive a call from a congregation to be ordained.) An interviewing committee, knowing that he was gay, told him he should consider doing something else with his life. He wondered at first if they might be right.

In 1994, Macdonald met with a search committee from St. Andrew's Presbyterian in Lachine. At the end of the interview, he told the committee that he was gay and that he and his partner, Chris Maragoudakis, lived together in a committed relationship. The committee discussed the matter and concluded that they still wanted him as their minister. The recommendation went to Session and unanimously from Session to the congregation, and he was invited to preach for a call. The Session talked personally with every member of the congregation. By the time of the congregational meeting to approve the call, everyone knew that Macdonald was gay. Ninety-four per cent of those present at the meeting voted in favour of the call. Presbytery approved the call, but he was never ordained. In an unprecedented move, a small group of presbyters lodged an appeal with the Presbyterian General Assembly (the highest decision-making body of the Presbyterian Church), which defeated the call. Macdonald continues to preach at St. Andrew's Presbyterian. He continues to give leadership, take funerals, offer pastoral care. The congregation warmly endorses him as their minister. He does everything but administer the sacraments.

So, six years after The Issue swept across the United Church, the folk at St. Andrew's United began to talk about these things with their Presbyterian cousins. Over coffee and between hands of cribbage, and in the kitchens at church socials, they talked about that openly gay minister. Said one person, "The people here at St. Andrew's United know Darryl. They know their friends at St. Andrew's Presbyterian love him. If you ask people if they'd have trouble with the issue of gay ordination, they'd probably have some difficulties, but they've had to talk about it in their kitchens. It's happened in our own backyard."

Two years later, it was time for St. Andrew's United to face the issue for themselves. In the summer of 1996, a lesbian couple came to church. They liked the welcome they received, they appreciated the friendly community. They were looking for a place to hold a ceremony to celebrate their commitment to each other. If they'd been heterosexual it would have been called a marriage. The minister took the request to the Session. At the meeting, one person was strongly opposed. Another elder said she didn't like the idea of a same-gender covenanting being held in her church, but she'd grown up in the United Church and knew the United Church's position. "If the church has said this is OK, they must have their reasons," she said. She chose to abstain. Everyone else was in favour.

The decision was announced in the church newsletter, so that people heard about it officially. There was very little reaction, no public outcry, no one left the church. The lesbian couple is still in the congregation and has become quite involved in congregational life. Their children are part of the Sunday school, and they are welcomed as a family at church events. People mostly refer to them as "the girls." They are, after all, quite a bit younger than the average member at St. Andrew's.

At the two St. Andrew's churches in Lachine, it seems that issues of homosexuality, viewed in abstract, might be too controversial to handle. But when it comes to people they know and like, well, people are people. The issue of same-gender covenants, looked at in abstract, would probably have been quite controversial and difficult to accept. As an issue or resolution, people would probably have turned it down. However, they could accept and value the relationship of two young newcomers, when they actually got to know them and their children as a family. Those things don't seem like such a big deal, not when it's part of your own community. Besides, they have other things to worry about right now. The bigger controversy at St. Andrew's United is dealing with an incident in which one of the church ladies got scalded in an accident at the spring tea. That required a special emergency meeting of the trustees. Then there's the fact that the strawberry social is only a week away and the strawberry crop is two weeks late!

At the General Council meeting in London, Ontario, in 1990 another group of commissioners from across the church reviewed the 1988 decision on sexual orientation and ministry. After carefully considering the flood of petitions from across the church, that General Council decided to uphold the decision. Many people wanted to put the whole issue of homosexuality and the church to rest, at least for awhile, but the United Church didn't get much breathing space. Only two years later, at the Halifax General Council in 1992, the church had to deal with a petition from Bloor St. United Church in Toronto asking it to "recognize and affirm the validity of same-gender covenants." Some people felt this was going too far. "Young people think they don't need marriage anymore," protested Adele Tucker, a commissioner to the 1992 Council from Sarnia, Ontario. "If we can't change something, we bless it."

When it came to a final decision, the United Church didn't say blessing of same-gender relationships couldn't be done. Neither did it give a clear directive mandating them. The 1992 General Council decided that more study was needed, resources for same-gender covenanting should be made available and, as with ordination and commissioning, it was up to each local congregation to decide what to do. Some congregations might affirm the validity of same-gender covenants, and others deny it. It was a fairly typical United Church compromise.

In reaching its decision, the 1992 General Council noted that in previous statements the church had recognized "the commitment present in relationships other than Christian marriage," and that "we are unclear about God's complete intention about human sexuality." Since then, many congregations have approved the celebration of same-gender covenants. The process hasn't always gone as smoothly as it did at St. Andrew's, Lachine.

Centenary-Queen Square United Church is in the old part of the city of St. John, New Brunswick. It has room for 1,200 people—the largest seating capacity of any church in St. John. About 65 people attend now on an average Sunday morning. It used to be Methodist, before the United Church came into being. In fact, it was the first Methodist church in Eastern Canada. It was also the first church in the Maritimes to have its Session approve a same-gender covenanting service.

Centenary-Queen Square says in its mission statement that it "seeks to be a sanctuary whereby through worship and service we become a place of safety for all people." In 1996, the congregation reaffirmed this mission and began a study process to look at what this actually means when you put it into practice. The Session named three significant groups of neighbours in the community around the church—abused women, poor people, and gays and lesbians—and began to meet with representatives of these groups to talk about what it might mean for the church to really be a place of welcome and safety for them.

It was during a discussion with gays and lesbians that the question of same-gender covenanting came up. It was raised by two members of the congregation, Jim Crooks and Carl Trickey. The couple had been considering having a celebration of commitment. Because of their life-long association with the church, they wanted to hold the ceremony in the Centenary-Queen Square sanctuary.

The Rev. Bob Johnson took the request to the Session. For him, this was simply a logical extension of the church's mission statement. "We have witnessed the love and affection these two have for each other," he said, "and it's a challenge for many of us in our own relationships." At the Session meeting, someone asked, "What does it mean?" Johnson replied that, in everyday language, "Jim and Carl are asking us if they can have their marriage celebrated in our sanctuary." There were a few questions about the United Church national policy. Someone asked cautiously, "This isn't going to be in the news is it?" and then there was a vote. There were eight in favour; one opposed. As one of the elders said, "I couldn't have done any differently because I had gotten to know these two men and saw their kindness, their goodness, their willingness to be a part of us. I've approved marriages and baptisms for people when I didn't have a clue who they were. And here are two people that I have gotten to know over a period of time and have appreciated their presence. How could I say no?"

The service took place in August 1996. Crooks' daughter read the scripture. Trickey's two boys were ring bearers. Family and friends joined in a wonderful celebration of love and commitment. Not everyone was supportive, however. The night before the service, someone painted graffiti on the church doors. The graffiti was removed within an hour, but the media got word of what was happening. CTV showed up with a reporter, and news of the event hit the St. John papers. There was a lot of opposition and outcry, more from the community than from within the congregation. There were quite a few letters to the editor, most of them not very supportive!

Things died down for a bit. Then Johnson got word that a petition was circulating in the congregation—a petition to have the Session's decision reversed. The petition called for a "declaration by the congregation that it did not approve of the use of its sanctuary for same-gender covenanting." Other parts of the building were OK. Use of the minister's time was OK. Just not in the sanctuary. A congregational meeting was called.

The meeting enjoyed the largest attendance at any meeting in the past 20 years. Johnson noticed there were "a number of people whom I had not met in the church in my whole time here, and I haven't seen them since." In his opinion, however, it was a good meeting. "It was very respectful. Everyone who wanted to express their opinion had a chance to do so. The discussion was very healthy." Johnson believes in letting people make their own decisions. He's seen too many congregations split in two "by clergy telling people what they should be saying and doing." Whatever his own opinions on the matter, he was able to lead the congregation in a process of fair and democratic decision making that left the congregation in a healthy state to continue to work together. It seems that the process by which decisions get made is, in the long run, at least as important as the outcome.

The petition against same-gender covenanting at Centenary-Queen Square was upheld, overturning the original decision of its Session. But the vote only carried by a very small margin. People pointed out that the 11 new members who joined the church in the following six months would have been enough to tip the balance. Several people who were key players in moving the petition forward later changed their minds on the issue; one, because a family member came out to him, another, because he heard Trickey speak at the meeting and had a chance to get to know him. Never mind, the motion had passed. It is history now and the congregation has moved on. Crooks and Trickey remain very active. Crooks is on the board of stewards. And there are several other gay and lesbian couples who attend regularly. They seem to feel they are welcome. In spite of the turmoil over same-gender covenanting, the congregation is a safe place for them to be who they are. And the congregation continues to work on its mission statement: being a place of welcome and safety for all.

Events at Centenary-Queen Square might not seem like a great leap forward in terms of social change. In fact, they illustrate how slow change really is—a few steps forward, a few back. But things like that can have a ripple effect. They get people talking. People in other churches in St. John Presbytery began discussing The Issue once more, The Issue that hadn't gone away. And, just when you think nothing's ever going to change, it does.

In 1988, immediately after the General Council decision, St. John Presbytery had passed a motion saying that its policy would be "not to knowingly accept into the candidacy process for recommendation for ordained ministry, commissioning, settlement or transfer any practicing homosexual or lesbian." In the midst of all the furor at Centenary-Queen Square, presbytery decided to take another look at the motion still on its books. And formally rescinded it. St. John Presbytery now says that sexual orientation is not a factor in determining whether a person should be supported in candidacy for ministry or settled or covenanted into a pastoral charge within the presbytery. Which is basically what the United Church decided, back in 1988.

5

SOMEONE WE KNOW

The facts of this world seen clearly are seen through tears; why tell me then there is something wrong with my eyes?

Margaret Atwood

"Judy" sat looking out the window at the swirling snow. She was impatient to get home. The receptionist had left already. The family practice clinic where she worked as a nurse was empty. The storm had prevented the doctor from getting in at all. Judy had reached most of the patients to tell them not to come, all but one. Since this was a new patient who lived some distance away, Judy decided to stick around just in case she showed up. She was just about to turn out the lights when "Amelia" arrived. As Judy explained the situation and suggested a time for another appointment, Amelia started sobbing.

Judy, a United Church member, had recently taken a lay training course on pastoral care. While they didn't exactly teach this in the course, Judy knew immediately that a cup of tea was in order. She plugged in the kettle, and the two women sat together in the empty waiting room. Judy listened, and Amelia told her story. Two years ago, Amelia's only son had told his parents that he was gay and that he had AIDS. When Amelia's husband heard of his son's illness, he immediately cut off all contact. He believed what their conservative Christian church was saying at the time, that homosexuality was a sin and AIDS was God's punishment. Her husband forbade Amelia ever to see her son again. He told all their friends that his son had died in a car accident.

Secretly, Amelia continued to see her son, to visit him and offer love and comfort through his last weeks and days. When he died, Amelia had no one to tell, no one with whom to share her grief, no one to witness her tears. So she made a doctor's appointment. With the doctor unavailable and unable to contain the secret any longer, Amelia poured out her story to a total stranger. For the first time, Amelia encountered someone who didn't think AIDS was God's punishment, someone who could affirm her love for her son and her grief at his tragic death. For Judy, AIDS and issues of sexual orientation acquired a human face: the face of a mother weeping for her sonSecretly, Amelia continued to see her son, to visit him and offer love and comfort through his last weeks and days. When he died, Amelia had no one to tell, no one with whom to share her grief, no one to witness her tears. So she made a doctor's appointment. With the doctor unavailable and unable to contain the secret any longer, Amelia poured out her story to a total stranger. For the first time, Amelia encountered someone who didn't think AIDS was God's punishment, someone who could affirm her love for her son and her grief at his tragic death. For Judy, AIDS and issues of sexual orientation acquired a human face: the face of a mother weeping for her son.

❧

D avid Hallman is an openly gay man who has worked for the national United Church in a variety of social justice portfolios since 1976. Hallman, who is himself HIV-positive, thinks the AIDS epidemic has helped, rather than hindered, the church's broader discussion of sexual orientation, because it touched people on an emotional level. He believes it's at that level, not at the rational or intellectual level, that real change in attitudes begins.

The AIDS epidemic began to surface in public consciousness in 1981. It was at this time that the United Church began talking in earnest about sexual orientation and ministry. Throughout all of The Issue years, AIDS was in people's minds. Hallman believes that AIDS and the theological debate in the United Church were interwoven. In 1985, the United Church initiated some important work on AIDS. At that time, according to Hallman, "the only theological or spiritual perspective being articulated on AIDS was one of judgement." Phrases like "God's punishment for gays" were bandied about in society. The United Church injected words of compassion into a negative and judgemental context.

The United Church's response, formulated in deliberate consultation with other churches, dealt with issues of public policy, education and pastoral care. In 1986, the General Council Executive approved the report, saying in part, "We affirm the Christian conviction that God loves and cares for all people, including persons with AIDS, and we reject the argument made by some that AIDS is God's punishment for homosexuals." The church lobbied for policies to end discrimination against people with HIV infection, urged federal and provincial governments to take action on the epidemic, and looked at ways the United Church could be "a supportive and effective ally in support of persons with AIDS." Many United Church congregations picked up the challenge to respond with compassion to the crisis on their doorsteps, giving pastoral care and support when AIDS hit close to home in one of their own members or members' families. Some embarked on special projects, helping to run shelters or hospices for people dying of HIV infection. Many became involved in education and advocacy, held vigils, participated in ecumenical worship services, or sponsored awareness projects like the AIDS Memorial Quilt. In the process of offering care and encountering real people, many United Church people took a second look at their own attitudes toward homosexuality.

Rosedale-Queen Mary United Church is a mid-sized congregation of about 175 families in Montreal. As its name suggests, it's a church that amalgamated two other congregations: Rosedale and Queen Mary Road. In 1988 there was quite a lot of discussion about The Issue at Queen Mary and there was a congregational vote on it. The congregation decided not to support the ordination of self-declared homosexuals. Rosedale United didn't debate quite so vigorously. There was only one congregational meeting, with no educational event beforehand. Mind you, there were some pretty powerful things said on both sides of the debate. Then people stopped talking about it and went on with other things.

Rosedale-Queen Mary United recently approved same-gender covenanting services as an official policy. According to the minister, the Rev. Shaun Fryday, there wasn't a large discussion. The issue didn't go to the whole congregation; it was dealt with by the board, whose members generally felt they didn't want to go through the same kind of big debate and discussion they'd had in 1988. Besides, the board does have a mandate to make those kinds of decisions on behalf of the congregation. "Normally, I don't bring wedding concerns before the congregation," Fryday says. However, he was quite surprised at the level of support. "Younger people, between 25 and 30 [years old] were saying 'why is this a question?' The people around my generation, in their forties, thought that we were already doing it, just because of 1988 and because society has changed so much." Fryday thinks the congregation is changing its attitudes—not rapidly, but changing nonetheless. Some of it is a generational thing, some of it may be because of changes in the society around it.

One of the significant indicators of change is the Rosedale-Queen Mary AIDS Project. Fryday doesn't think this kind of project could have happened in the congregation 10 years ago. It has been very successful, bringing different constituencies and different communities together to work on education, support and advocacy. The project holds community forums to educate members of the congregation and other clergy about the AIDS crisis, and does joint fund raising to support a centre for women and children with AIDS. It sponsored a vigil on World AIDS Day. The project also has a support group for family and friends of people who are gay. They are working on a professional training day for clergy and lay people who are encountering people affected by HIV and AIDS. They hope this will enable other congregations to set up their own community-based groups and support programs. Fryday preached about the project one Sunday. "People feel this is the kind of ministry they are called to be about," he said. Then he urged other members of the congregation to find their particular calling to ministry and "get on with it."

AIDS helped United Church people see clearly the hatred being projected against many gay people. More importantly, perhaps, it introduced people to a side of the gay community they had not seen before. Says United Church minister, the Rev. Craig Chaplin, "The plague brought out the very best in terms of the compassion, fortitude, caring and integrity of our relationships, both individually and collectively. The overwhelming pastoral care that our community has poured into caring for brothers and sisters with AIDS has been phenomenal. And it has been visible. It is a beautiful story and it continues to unfold. It's hard to estimate the impact of that as a witness to the power of same-sex love." Families, friends and the medical community have witnessed that story, at bedsides, in hospital waiting rooms, in clinics, on the streets. Chaplin thinks it has helped a lot of people to park their homophobia for a time, if not get rid of it altogether.

One example of this kind of shift in attitudes showed up in a training event for lay pastoral ministers. Lay pastoral ministers in the United Church are lay people who receive specialized training to do congregational ministry often in very isolated communities where there aren't a lot of ordained folk around. Most of them come from the very small communities they now serve as ministers. They are in touch with the grass roots, because they are the grass roots. It's a big deal for lay pastoral ministers from very small communities to go to a major city like Montreal, as they do for training events.

In the summer of 1997, 30 of them gathered for an educational session on theology and pastoral care. A chaplain from one of the large city hospitals was their resource person. He works a lot with people who are HIV-infected, many of whom are gay. He told the group of the "constant conversion" that happens for him through these encounters. On one occasion, he was called to the bedside of a man with AIDS. The man's partner was there. The two had lived together for 25 years and now one of them was dying. They asked the chaplain to marry them. The lay pastoral ministers listened intently as the chaplain told them the story. Without finishing his account of the incident, the chaplain turned the question over to the group. "What would you do in this situation?" he asked them. "Would you marry them?" Small groups went off to discuss it. When they reconvened, two people still seem to be thinking about it, perhaps still undecided. The other 28 said they would marry the couple without question. They weren't quite sure what it would mean legally, or even theologically, but pastorally, they knew what was needed in this situation. As one person in the group put it, "It does something in my gut, something inside me says 'yes.' I don't know how I could do anything else."

AIDS forced many gay men out of the closet. A lot of United Church people came to know gays within their immediate circle of family and friends. Often, these disclosures were life-affirming points of connection and learning. When Chaplin came out as a gay person with HIV infection, a whole congregation had a human face, someone they knew and loved, to replace stereotypes and misconceptions.

Chaplin was ordained in 1980, in an era when "don't ask, don't tell" seemed the norm for gay and lesbian candidates. "I don't even remember contemplating coming out as a serious option," he recalls. "With anyone I did tell in those early years, the response was always the same: don't rock the boat and everything will be fine." He went to enormous lengths to hide his sexual orientation and his relationship from his first congregation. His partner never answered the phone. He could only enter the house through the back door. If anyone came to the door he went upstairs immediately. The pressure was horrendous. "I needed to believe people didn't know he was in the house," Chaplin explains. "We managed to eke out a life, but it was very stressful."

In 1984, he moved to Union United Church in Ste. Anne de Bellevue, near Montreal. In 1986, when the congregation studied the issue, they invited a "real gay person" to come and talk to them. It was ironic. They could have talked to their minister, if anyone had known. By 1988, Chaplin had come out to a number of key people in the congregation, but most still were not aware of his sexual orientation. A commissioner to the 1988 General Council, he sat in the auditorium, a closeted gay, HIV-positive man. When he joined in the debate, he spoke carefully, in the third person.

Chaplin's deteriorating health finally forced him to go public. In 1992, he stood in front of his congregation and told them who he was. He would have preferred to come out in different circumstances but knows that, but for AIDS, he might never have done so. "I'm grateful that if I had to develop HIV, at least it became a catalyst for the kind of growth and change I needed to do," he says. It became a very life-affirming opportunity to claim his life back both from the closet and the disease. He feels both were deadly. "In many ways, the closet was killing me faster than the virus, spiritually if not physically, because of the enormous pressure I felt to conform outwardly to an image that wasn't who I was."

Chaplin recognizes the cost of all those years of speaking in the third person, answering evasively. As closets go, it wasn't too uncomfortable. He had come out to a lot of people in the congregation, but that just meant they, too, were part of the web of silence. "I may be feeling more liberated but, really, all I've done is broadened the web of deceit. I have brought them into my closet. But they haven't brought me out into the sunshine. It was quite different the day I stood up in a public forum and said, 'This is who I am.' Because, at that point, I wasn't inviting them into the closet, I was knocking the door down." Chaplin regrets that it had to be done under those kind of circumstances. "In the best of all possible worlds, it's not the kind of script I would have written," he says. "But given the hand I was dealt, I did the best I could."

Bonnie Norris has been church secretary at Union since 1982. Her connection with the congregation goes back more than 30 years, and she knows it inside out. "Craig had virtually 99 per cent support from the congregation," she believes. He was well liked and well respected for his enabling and empowering style of leadership. As Norris sees it, the major problem was not the fact that he was gay but that he was leaving the congregation, and that he was going to be leaving ministry. "That upset people considerably," she says.

One or two families had left Union United over The Issue in 1988. Most had more or less accepted that this was where the United Church stood, but many were still uncomfortable with homosexuality. For many in the congregation, Chaplin was the first openly gay person they had ever met. Lynn Thompson, her husband and their three children were all very involved members at Union. The children were teenagers at the time of Chaplin's announcement and departure. Thompson acknowledges that she used to be very uncomfortable with the idea of homosexuals in ministry. Her own parents had very conservative views, and she didn't really get involved in the discussions the church was having in 1988. Now that she knows someone personally, she sees the issue very differently. "We're not just talking about this term 'homosexuals' anymore. I always see Craig. He was a wonderful minister, and it put a very personal face on the issue. The whole issue of homosexuality in the church will be forever coloured by the fact that we know Craig."

The Thompson children all supported Chaplin and his ministry. Alison was in Chaplin's last confirmation class at Union. Alison is now 21, just graduating from social work studies at McGill. She has been very active at Union. At 19, she was elected an elder, and became the youngest member of Session. She always had a lot of admiration for her minister. "He was an incredible speaker," she says. "He had a way of getting through to the younger people of the church. He was down-to-earth, and he was approachable. He was a very positive role model."

Alison recalls the shock she felt at Chaplin's announcement. She was 15 at the time, and had only heard the word 'homosexual' occasionally at school. It wasn't something talked about much in the small community of Ste. Anne. "I had no idea that he was gay, and I didn't know anyone else who was. I had heard of HIV and I was very worried for him."

She now thinks that knowing Chaplin prevented her from ever developing negative stereotypes about homosexuality. It had a lot to do with knowing him for a few years before she knew he was gay. "I didn't think of him just as a 'gay man.' He was a dear friend, a minister, and he was gay. I was blessed by this being my introduction to homosexuality. That was the best way to have broken me into this new community of which I was totally unaware. If I hadn't had that experience, I'd be a very different person."

Alison now makes a point of bringing up the topic of homosexuality in her wider family, not all of whom see the issue as she does. "Even before I started social work studies, I was very opinionated," she confesses. At first, she had a hard time talking about it because she got so angry. "Everyone would be upset. My grandmother would come right out and say, 'Maybe I'm just old fashioned, but they have no business in church.' My mother would kind of take a look at me. She'd squeeze my hand ... I wouldn't have felt so strongly if I hadn't been through that experience with Craig. I had grounds to argue, 'you're wrong!'"

Alison's generation is different from that of her parents. There's more peer pressure to support homosexuality, and she has many friends who are gay or lesbian. There are more role models, more out gays and lesbians in her church, community and world. "My particular friends may be a bit more aware than other people my age, but that's the way it is to be supportive," she says. Alison admits she's still occasionally working on her grandparents, "but not at major holidays!"

6

YOUTH: THE FUTURE PRESENT

Learn from those who are older than you; learn from your contemporaries; and never cease to learn from your children.

Margaret Laurence.

Nine-year-old Allison is having a birthday party with eight of her friends. They are sitting around the kitchen table eating birthday cake and chattering away. Allison's mother is clearing away a few dishes. The girls talk on, oblivious to her presence.

"Did you know that Katie has two moms?" asks one of Allison's guests.

"Yeah, I knew that. They're lesbians," another girl declares.

"I think that's gross!" says Allison.

Allison's mother stops what she is doing. She is just about to intervene, to say something about prejudice, about respecting people who are different. She doesn't need to. The other girls have already challenged Allison.

"What do you mean, 'it's gross'?" one of them demands. "People can have two moms, or two dads. There's nothing wrong with that!"

"Yeah," say several others. Allison's peers remind her that not everyone is the same. People are people, even gays and lesbians. Then the conversation moves on to other things. Allison's mother goes back to the sink, wondering at how much has changed. She knows kids still use words like "lezzie" and "queer" and "homo" to insult one another. She knows that the world can still be a brutal place for a lesbian or gay young person. Yet, here in her own kitchen is a group of nine year olds willing to challenge bigotry and speak up in defence of a friend who has two moms. They use words with naturalness and ease—words that, at their age, she never even knew existed. There has been quite a change in a few short years.

❦

"Clare" picks up her physics text and tries to concentrate on studying. She canhear her younger brothers' high-pitched voices in the back ground, arguingover the best way to beat a certain character in a computer game. "I give up!" she exclaims, flopping onto her bed and pulling out the latest copy of *Xtra!*, a gay/lesbian community newspaper, from under the bed. Clare, who is 16 and in her final year of high school, is in the process of telling her family and friends that she is lesbian. The first person she told was her best friend. She wrote to her while her friend was away as a camp counsellor. The letter that came in reply was one of the nicest she has ever received. "I wish I were there so I could give you a great big hug," wrote her friend. Clare has lots of support, but still finds the process of coming out a bit tricky. "The thing with having such a supportive family is that it's kind of weird," she says. "It's weird because everyone just assumes ... well, it's hard to know how to tell them 'officially.'"

She hears someone calling her from downstairs. She gathers up her school papers and glances around the room. The copy of *Xtra!* is still lying open on the bed. Undecided, she stands in the middle of the room, until her name is called once again. She isn't quite out to everyone ... yet. Deliberately, she turns and leaves the room.

She knew at the time she didn't really need to hide herself or her sexuality. "My parents have now know officially for at least a year. Even having a really supportive family, I still went through a phase when I was hiding everything. I was reading all the gay and lesbian stuff I could get my hands on, and someone would ask 'What are you reading?' 'Oh, nothing.' Mom asked me, but not directly. She said, 'I know what you're reading, if you want to tell me or want any information ... until then I'll leave it to you.'"

Clare knows her family would be there for her if she ever needed to talk. Many of her parents' friends are lesbian or gay, and they attend a United Church that is openly affirming of the gay and lesbian communities. The congregation is fairly small, and very involved in social justice in the downtown. A couple of years ago it became an Affirming Congregation, a congregation that has undertaken a study process and has decided to welcome and include gay, lesbian and bisexual people in all aspects of its life and work. Clare recalls that process. "The day of the actual service when we officially became an Affirming Congregation, was on my birthday. It was a really great service!" she declares with enthusiasm. "Everyone was really excited. It seemed like a big party, but there was also a lot of meaning for a lot of people. There are many gay and lesbian couples in our congregation, so it was really positive for them. It was a way of saying who we are as a community." For her personally it was significant because the church has been a community where she has made a lot of close adult friends. "It is important for me that my church is welcoming of all people," she says. "Having church where it was an Affirming Congregation, and all the events that happened, means it's never been the case that I've had no one to talk to or had no place to go."

Clare has been very involved in church all her life. Last year, she co-chaired a stewardship committee with her dad, and is now chairing it. She has been on six other committees in the congregation. She's also very active in youth-at-Conference programs. The issue of sexual orientation comes up occasionally with Conference youth, but "generally it's a non-issue," she says. "The people who attend are really open-minded; very few are conservative. There were some people within that program who were openly gay or lesbian and that was sort of an accepted fact. It wasn't a big 'Oh my gosh!' One day someone wore this T-shirt which was a spoof on all the comments made about gay people. No one questioned it. It was just like, OK, that's who he is."

Clare has only experienced a church that is welcoming of gays and lesbians. She never heard messages of condemnation and judgement from her church, messages that some older people spend lifetimes trying to get over. The message she grew up with is that, in her church, it's OK to be who she is. She was eight in 1988, and doesn't recall hearing anything about The Issue. "Until last year I don't think I really knew that all that stuff had happened, that it was such a great big issue," she says. "I just assumed that the whole church was ready to become Affirming Congregations." It has made growing up, and coming out, a lot easier.

Even with the changes that have taken place in church and society, not all youth today find themselves in such a supportive environment. Gay and lesbian youth struggle, even more than other youth, to find themselves in a culture hostile to homosexuality. This can be a terrible burden at a critical time in their lives. Each year in the United States about 5,000 young people between the ages of 15 and 24 take their own lives. According to the U.S. Department of Health and Human Services, at least 30 per cent of those suicides are directly related to the individual's struggle with his or her sexual orientation. Groups working with gay and lesbian youth in Canada say that although there are no comparable Canadian studies, the statistics here are very similar. Between 30 and 40 per cent of runaway and homeless American youth are lesbian, gay or bisexual, write Kate Bass and Kate Kaufman in *Free Your Mind: The book for gay, lesbian and bisexual youth—and their allies*. Sixty per cent of gay men and 30 per cent of lesbians report being physically or verbally attacked at some time during their student years.

In the midst of that difficult reality, youth struggle with such basic questions as: What's wrong with me? How do I know if I'm really gay? What should I tell my parents? Sometimes they turn to the church for answers, for help and support. One ordained United Church minister describes how the topic came up in her youth group: "We were preparing a youth-led worship service, and the kids were raising all sorts of things they wanted to include—a lot of issues, like violence, peace, the environment, things they really care a lot about. Then someone said 'AIDS.' There was kind of a lull in the conversation; everything stopped. After a moment someone else asked, 'What does the church think about homosexuality?' It was funny in a way, because I'd just assumed they'd all know that. Then I realized, none of them had really been involved in all those discussions in 1988. Some of them were still in kindergarten. So I told them about the policy and what the church had said about human rights and stuff, that the church didn't condemn homosexuality. They were really surprised. About a week later, a member of the group came to talk to me..." Hearing the United Church's position can be crucial in a young person's life. For those inside the United Church as well as outside it, the church's voice is very significant.

Allison Rennie also was raised in a United Church environment. At 36, she's old enough to remember a different church—a church with no Affirming Congregations, a church still struggling to define who was included and who wasn't. When she agreed to be a lesbian resource person to Sessional Committee Eight at the 1988 General Council, she says, she didn't think she was agreeing to have herself named in the national media, "Allison Rennie, the lesbian resource to the sessional committee...

"Oh well," she says now, with a shrug. "It felt like being outed in the national press. On the other hand, anyone who had observed my life would probably have thought I was lesbian anyway. It wasn't like my job was at stake. I was already out to friends and family, so no one close was harmed by that."

Rennie, who is a staff person with British Columbia Conference working with youth and young adults, recalls the struggles of that General Council year, and realizes how much has changed. "Before 1988 the church was a really different place. It's a really different experience for me now, 10 years later," she declares. "One of the indicators is that I am out, I am working for the church in a visible and public way with youth, and people aren't fainting." It seems not to be an issue and she believes she would be hearing about it if it were. "It does not inhibit my work, not at all," she says. "I don't have proof that everyone knows but I have made absolutely no secret about it. I work in all sorts of different communities in B.C. and lots of people from those communities speak openly about my relationship. My own ability to exercise my ministry and to share my gifts and leadership is in part due to my ability to be honest with people and to be out. I don't live in fear of losing my job."

She notes that the context for youth and young adults has changed considerably since 1988, when she was a young adult. Today the acceptance of people who are gay, lesbian and bisexual is much higher. "I know a number of young adults who have gone out with people of the same sex and that seems to be fairly generally known and not a big deal," notes Rennie. She thinks that is, in part, a result of what the church has done, but also relates it to the fact that Vancouver, where she lives, is a fairly liberal city.

Although it hasn't gone away, the blatant prejudice doesn't seem as prevalent, particularly among youth and young adults. Rennie notices that more and more young people speak up about justice issues for gays and lesbians. She tells of a young adult at a table group at General Council in 1997. "She listened as another commissioner, an adult, was absolutely blowing his stack about same-gender benefits and the definition of spouse in the Income Tax Act." The young adult clearly supported the petition and was really surprised that anyone would find it offensive. "That a person would be surprised by that kind of attitude says that there is a lot more general acceptance," says Rennie. She finds that a lot more youth have gay and lesbian friends in school. "They are very aware of the persecution in the high school setting and deeply feel that that's wrong. That is way, way, different from when I was in high school!" It's even a change from 10 years ago. There's no question that the attitudes of youth are different from those of previous generations. And many of them are taking leadership to continue to push for change, and to ensure that gay and lesbian rights are respected, both inside and outside the church.

The face of the Christian church is quite conservative in Abbotsford, in British Columbia's Fraser Valley. Some say it's the province's equivalent of the Bible belt. A young adult in his late twenties who lives there and is gay realized that there was a desperate need for some place where gay, lesbian and bisexual youth could meet. So he established a group called Youth Quest and began to seek funding to get it on its feet. One of his friends who was involved in young adult networks in the United Church suggested that Youth Quest apply to the Van Dusen Fund, which is administered by British Columbia Conference. The proposal was accepted and while it was not a great deal of money in proportion to the program's overall budget, it showed the United Church was supportive and involved. That led to all kinds of "interesting" press, especially out in the Fraser Valley, recalls Rennie. "Those youth and young adults were clearly high risk. Because of their sexuality and their sense of being so marginalized they turn to things like alcohol, drugs and street life as an outlet from that very repressive environment," she says. Rennie is proud that the church would support youth in that way. "I thought that press was good for us as a church," she adds. In the meantime, the Youth Quest organization has had so much interest that it has opened several other centres in the Valley.

Svend Robinson, NDP MP for Burnaby-Douglas, was Canada's first openly gay Member of Parliament. He came out in 1988, shortly before the United Church General Council, and was re-elected later that same year. Robinson thinks the leadership that youth are giving is "the single most exciting and most hopeful development for gay, lesbian and bisexual communities." He applauds the tremendous strength of young people, "gutsy out high school students who are not going to take any rubbish from anyone. What's happening in schools is one of the most important battlegrounds because that is where people's attitudes are shaped. That's where we have to confront homophobia." There, and in other places, youth are bringing changes.

One United Church Conference youth program decided it would form itself into an "affirming committee," one that welcomes and includes all. Members of the program have begun to talk about how they can change their language and structures to ensure gay and lesbian youth feel explicitly welcomed and accepted. Youth also are speaking up in their congregations. One minister recalls a church debate over whether or not the congregation should begin to explore becoming an Affirming Congregation. An adult objected to the idea of the church talking about this issue all over again, saying it would stir up unnecessary conflict. A 15 year old rose to speak. "Wait a minute," he said. "You talk about the church being like a family. Families are able to talk about anything, to be honest with each other without worrying about where the discussion is going to take them. I think we should talk about this issue."

Not content to leave things as the church left them in 1988, youth continue to push the conversation, challenging the church to continue to grow and change. Gen Creighton has spent the past two years in youth ministry. Now 24, she recently graduated from university and is heading off to Guatemala to work on women's and children's programs with the Christian Task Force on Central America. Creighton has been active in Conference youth and young adult ministry for many years, beginning at age 15 when she attended the 1988 General Council as a youth delegate. At one point in her life she had a youth leader who was lesbian. Creighton thought she was the greatest thing that ever walked on earth! She grew up in a family whose commitment to justice work gave her strong values of justice and inclusion. She says the leader and her family combined to "make me passionately angry at any who would dare to exclude someone because of their sexual orientation." She went into the 1988 General Council a strong advocate of lesbians and gays, and felt proud of the church afterward. "I didn't think the church would ever choose to ordain gays and lesbians as the debate was going on," she says. "But I was still angry because I thought everyone should believe what I believed." These days she may not be quite so adamant as she was in 1988, but she still has lots of energy and commitment for The Issue. She thinks the church has more to learn.

"I don't think that the church has come that far yet in terms of looking at sexuality as a continuum rather than as boxes," she explains. "The church has become more accepting of gays and lesbians but hasn't had the full discussion around the whole range of sexuality and the places of grey in the middle and I think the church still needs to discuss that.

"People can deal with you if you were 'born that way'—you can't help the way you are so we might as well accept your gifts. But what about saying people make choices about how they live out their sexuality? That requires a greater leap of imagination than accepting that you were born that way. I would consider myself to be bisexual. In my experience, gender is not a criteria for somebody to love. If I fall in love with someone it won't be because they are male or female necessarily; it will be because of their personality and how they live and all sorts of other things."

Creighton thinks the church needs to start listening more to young people about their experiences, and that it needs to continue to talk about sexuality. "I think it's really important for youth to be able to make the connection between sexuality and spirituality," she declares. "Where else can you hear the discussion of the spiritual and sexuality together? It doesn't happen in other parts of society. We need to start having that conversation again and it needs to happen with new voices. We need to frame the whole discussion differently than we did in 1988. I don't want to negate the work that has come before in terms of advocacy for gays and lesbians, but I don't think that is where we need to be right now. But the opportunity for having this conversation is based on the work of really courageous people and their ability to speak out and change the church." Creighton has a vision of where that conversation might lead the church. It's one of the things she intends to work on as soon as she gets back from Guatemala.

7

CHOOSING TO CHANGE

Life is either a daring adventure or nothing. Security does not exist in nature, nor do the children of [humanity] as a whole experience it. Avoiding danger is no safer in the long run than exposure.

Helen Keller

Historically speaking, when human beings are faced with the choice between destruction and change, they are apt to choose change, and it's about the only thing that will make them choose change.

Peace Pilgrim

It is time for the children's conversation at First United Church in Ottawa. Thirty or so children and youth scurry forward to find a spot to sit at the front. They are not particularly quiet. In this congregation, children are seen and heard. This month, children's conversations are being led by lay people. The young man who greets them knows the children well; he taught many of them in the primary Sunday school class, and they are comfortable chatting with him. In the course of the conversation he mentions his partner by name. It's not a big deal that his partner happens to be a man. It doesn't need to be. Everyone has known for years that he is gay. The children's story ends, and the children burst out of the sanctuary, off to Sunday school.

The next week, it's a lesbian woman who leads the children's conversation. Again, her relationship is as natural a part of the conversation as the discussion the children have with her about planting gardens. Next week, this time will be led by a single parent and his teenage son. It's all part of the mix at First United Church.

❧

First United Church hasn't always been so lively. It hasn't always been as open about issues of sexual orientation. Nor have people who are gay and lesbian always been so visible within the community. The congregation has undergone a transformation many years in the making. In the early '80s it was one of a number of aging, inner-city congregations. Upkeep of its old, stone building was a huge drain on the sparse resources of a dwindling membership, many of whom now lived outside of the immediate neighbourhood. Virtually no young families were attending. Presbytery was seriously considering closing the congregation, but decided to give it one last chance, says the Rev. Sharon Moon. Moon was settled there with a clear mandate: to help restore the congregation to life or to help it die with dignity. She was very clear with members of the congregation about the things they needed to do to survive. They needed to understand their sense of who they were as a congregation and why they were there—their mission as a congregation. They needed to be open and welcoming to newcomers and the changes that newcomers brought. And they had to be open to the movement of the Spirit in their midst. In other words, they had to change. Or die.

The congregation rose to the challenge and declared itself ready for change, but no one could have anticipated the depth and breadth of change that might be coming. The debate about the issue of sexual orientation and ministry was as hot in Ottawa Presbytery as it was anywhere. Many people at First United Church weren't at all comfortable with the idea of homosexuals being admitted into ministry. In 1988, for the sake of congregational peace, they decided not to send in a petition to General Council. They were afraid that declaring a position would divide and potentially even demolish a congregation already feeling fragile because of low membership and shaky finances. Moon encouraged congregational members to express themselves, within a climate where all views were respected. She recognized that there was a wide range of opinion at First United, and didn't believe in silencing people. She herself was right in the thick of the debate in other courts of the church, however, making clear her strong support for gay and lesbian people, and for gays and lesbians in ministry. The media were covering the debate very closely, and Moon was quoted several times in the local press. Her vibrant presence and strong convictions, not only about issues of sexual orientation but on other issues as well, began to attract newcomers to First United.

Jack Stewart has been a member of First United all his life. In the 1980s, he was serving both as Clerk of Session and presbytery representative, and he was one of the people determined to see First survive. He made a point of welcoming newcomers personally and getting to know them.

For most of his 75 years Stewart had believed that homosexuality was a sin and a perversion. That was, until he met Bill Siksay and Brian Burke. The couple had come to Ottawa to work—both were assistants to MPs at the time—and started attending First United. Stewart got to know them, and he was deeply impressed by their spirituality, their commitment and the leadership they offered their temporary church home. In 1988, Stewart stood up at a meeting of Ottawa Presbytery to speak about the issue of sexual orientation and ministry. "I was wrong," he said. He told about meeting a gay couple in his congregation and of the gifts that they brought to his home church. Seeing their loving relationship and their deep faith had made him change his mind, he said. As with so many others, meeting someone and getting to know them personally made all the difference.

Reta Rogers lives on a quiet, tree-lined street in an Ottawa suburb. Her husband, now retired, was in the navy for 35 years. His work took him out of town many months of the year. She stayed home to raise their two daughters, both now in their twenties. Rogers was introduced to First United when one of her daughters was a social work student working in a summer job at a group home for recovering addicts. Moon offered a spiritual presence at the group home. "My daughter was so impressed with the work Sharon was doing and said we'd probably be happy at First United," Rogers explains.

Rogers had tried a few other churches, and never really felt included. Apart from teaching Sunday school, she hadn't had a lot of church involvement in her adult years. She liked the friendly welcome she received at First United, and quickly became involved there. It was only as the issue of sexual orientation started to be discussed in the congregation that she noticed that gay and lesbian people also had started coming to the church because of what they had heard about its minister. "It was only after The Issue started to be raised," she explains, "that we realized there were a number of them there."

She didn't find this easy at first, having been raised in a very strict Presbyterian home. She and her husband even considered finding another church. She had known only one gay man before. "I certainly felt they were over there, and we were over here!" she describes her attitude at the time.

However, Rogers is not the sort to back away from issues she finds uncomfortable. She is direct, asks questions, and is open to other points of view. She talked to Moon. And she talked to the retired Anglican priest who lives next door to her and discovered, to her surprise, "that I couldn't see his narrow point of view. I just believe you have to accept people as people." Gradually she began to meet and get to know people in the congregation who were lesbian or gay. She realized they were just people, who lived their lives every day just as she did. Some of them were raising children, just as she had. She began to see "the tremendous love they had for each other." Seeing that, she started to realize "this cannot be anything but good." Still, she struggled with what she had learned in her Presbyterian upbringing, and with her own genuine questions about morality, about what's right and what's wrong in the area of human sexuality.

Rogers was clear on other parts of the Christian message, however, and in particular had a strong sense of the importance of caring for others in need. Shortly after she came to First United, she began to volunteer at the local food bank. Spending time at an inner-city food bank was as big an eye-opener as meeting gays and lesbians, she says. She still picks up food, gets to know people who use the service and "whines"—the word she uses to describe her persistent requests for donations from the congregation. She came to be known as someone who gets things done, and she was asked to be an elder. Her initial response was, "I'm not holy enough." She was thinking about the elders in the church where she grew up, "the staunch old men who always came to church, and looked at you sideways if you smiled." She thought it over, though, and agreed to give it a try.

Rogers wasn't the only one at First United struggling with the issue of sexual orientation and the presence of some newcomers who were open about their sexual orientation. Opinions were divided, and feelings high, when the congregation received a request in October 1991 to permit a same-gender covenanting between two lesbian members.

Moon conveyed the request to the Session, launching what she describes as "a very powerful process. It was a movement of the Spirit," she says. "The request enabled two lesbians to come out. And our whole community made a choice to risk faithfulness and solidarity." Rogers attended that Session meeting. "I remember sitting there absolutely frozen," she recalls. "I'd never even thought about such a thing. I thought it was ridiculous." One of the other elders said, "Let's not go ahead with this right now. We can't do this to our members." Rogers went home and said to her husband, "I don't want to be part of this. I don't like it at all!"

Session eventually concluded that because the request had such enormous implications for the congregation, it needed to be dealt with by the official board. The board, in turn, decided to consult the whole congregation. In good United Church fashion, a committee was established to help steer the process of reflection and discussion. It was a mixed group, composed of people who were supportive, people who weren't, and at least one person who was openly gay.

RD was part of that committee. She wasn't out when she started. "I can honestly say that my involvement in that process was one of the highlights of my life so far, in that it meant coming out to the congregation," she says. "Even though, for what are good personal reasons, I am not willing to be out absolutely everywhere, I nevertheless have found this to be the third most-liberating experience of my life."

RD had attended the United Church with her family as a child, though she admits she went mainly for the music. She enjoyed singing in choirs. She was confirmed at the age of 16, but fell away from regularly attending when she went to college. She had her reasons. "By then I had a pretty clear idea which way my orientation was inclining and I figured that would not fly as far as God was concerned," she says. "I don't know why I thought that, but I was convinced. I guess I was pinning my own homophobia on God." Looking back, she can't point to any one really bad experience; it's just that the whole culture was so negative. And, of course, she never received any positive messages for who she really was. "How could I? I was so busy trying to fade into the woodwork. If black is the absence of colour, then I'd say my negativity towards myself was the absence in my mind of any hope of acceptance from any quarter."

By the time 1988 rolled around, RD was starting to feel better about herself. She had kicked what she calls "a couple of self-destructive habits" and was established in a career she enjoyed. She had a very small circle of gay friends with whom she and her partner could socialize. A few years earlier she had come out, either deliberately or inadvertently, to a couple of straight friends and family members, with mixed results. "Nothing that would encourage me to repeat the experience," is how she puts it.

She was also starting to feel more comfortable in her relationship with God, a process that had developed "over nearly a decade of sitting in church basements around town." She was starting to get curious about what went on in the sanctuaries. At the same time, she was astonished and delighted to read in a stray copy of *The United Church Observer* that the United Church was grappling openly with the issue of recognizing gays and lesbians in their midst, "recognizing that we, as much as anyone else, have gifts to bring to the church." She began to wonder about giving some support to the United Church, and if she was going to support it, why not attend it.

The time had come to find herself a church. RD began attending First United in the summer of 1990. She had heard that there were a couple of gay men who went there, and she knew the congregation had "given the issue some thought." She discovered a congregation made up of all kinds of people, of all ages—a place that seemed to welcome and celebrate diversity, a place that would welcome her!

RD became more and more active at First, and was soon elected an elder. At Session she first began to speak out about issues of sexual orientation, and to come out herself. Meanwhile, Rogers had decided to go a step further in her own attempts to come to terms with the issue of sexual orientation. She invited RD, a woman her own age, to come for supper. RD accepted. The two women shared a meal and they talked. The conversation began with Rogers saying to her guest, in her typically forthright fashion, "so tell me why you think this is right." Then Rogers listened, really listened, as RD talked about her life and her relationship with a woman she calls "my beloved." The conversation lasted several hours, and by the end, Rogers had changed her mind.

Meanwhile, the committee charged with responsibility for taking discussion forward in the congregation met and began to work out a process for getting the congregation involved. The issue was very threatening for many—for closeted gays and lesbians fearful they would lose a supportive community, for people openly homophobic, for adults who had experienced abuse as children, for open gays and lesbians fearful they might lose the support of a congregation they had grown to love. "There were all these pastoral care needs," says Moon. "At the same time, it was incredibly healing for many people."

The congregation held what they called a day of discernment to discuss the request for a same-gender covenanting service and its implications. "We were setting a precedent," said Norman Ball, then Clerk of Session. "Whatever we decided on this one request would be our policy." Study kits and a copy of the letter were given to all members. People were invited to pray, and questions for personal reflection were provided. Several "meet a gay and lesbian" gatherings were held to help build congregational awareness.

The discernment day itself began with Sunday morning worship, Taizé-style, with lots of silence and no sermon. "There was no preaching about the issue," said Moon, "just an invitation to listen to the Spirit." People met over lunch to review First United's mission statement, talk about what members valued about the congregation, and hear a history of the process. This was not a day to take a vote, it was a day to listen. The official board would make the decision, according to United Church policy, but it would be informed by this day. The discernment process then continued with information about covenanting ceremonies, including reading a liturgy from a recent ceremony.

A crucial element of the process was the sharing of losses and opportunities. Not pro and con or for and against, these were lists the congregation compiled of things that might be lost and gained, whichever way the decision went. Everyone, regardless of his or her opinion, was invited to share in compiling these lists. This process broke down barriers. People who supported the request named some of the potential losses for those who were opposed. People who were opposed were able to see opportunities for the congregation in a decision they did not support. There were moments of pain, moments of anger, signs of struggle, and always a sense of the presence of the Spirit as the congregation paused frequently through the meeting for silent prayer.

In March 1992, the official board met to make its final decision. It voted—17 for, 6 opposed—"to accept the proposal for the performance of holy union ceremonies at First United Church between same-sex couples." The board noted that space was still needed to respect differing points of view, and the criteria would have to be developed. The current policy is that the same guidelines apply as those used for heterosexual weddings. No one left the church over this. Even those who disagreed with the final decision acknowledged that they felt heard and respected in their opinions. Many say that the process itself—the care, the length of time, the building of trust, the intentional listening—was what made it possible for the congregation to make the decision it did, and still hold together as a congregation in spite of the disagreements that remained.

The decision and the discernment process had a tremendous impact. According to Moon, it "has influenced everything we've done since. It has given us a model for decision making, a model for dealing with differences." RD is still an elder at First United. "The discernment process and the outcome set off a ripple effect that is still going on six years later," she says. "I have a sense that, in our congregation, the lions and the lambs are at ease with each other." There are signs that the congregation has learned to accept, even to welcome, the diversity of its membership.

It's time for the spring tea, an annual tradition at First United for as long as anyone can remember. Women are scurrying about with teacups and trays of cakes and sandwiches. Those honoured with the task of pouring are seated behind the silver tea pots. A couple of them are wearing extravagant, wide-brimmed hats adorned with flowers. At a quick glance, it looks as though the church has stepped back in time. Ironically, this occasion may be a leap forward. This tea is jointly sponsored by the United Church Women (average age 70 plus) and the First United Church Lesbian Potluck Group, a somewhat younger group of women, mostly in their forties and fifties. The lesbian women volunteered to help with the tea when they realized that the UCW was somewhat short-staffed. Reta Rogers received the offer to help as "the best news I've heard in a long time!" The UCW have found their energies flagging a bit in recent years.

Women from the lesbian potluck group, which meets monthly for a potluck supper, have baked cookies and squares along with everyone else. They help serve tea and take turns washing up. Many of their friends have come to the tea, along with the usual, somewhat-more-traditional crowd. A local feminist choir, "Womensing," provides some musical entertainment.

Rogers is in the kitchen, making sure things flow smoothly. There's been a problem with the coffee being a bit cool. "I think you're the only straight woman in here," one of the other women teases her. "I don't mind if you don't," she quips back. Everyone laughs.

One of the other UCW women reported on the tea in church the following week, thanking the lesbian group for its support. The tea had been a fabulous success, she declared. It had generated more money than any tea, ever, in the entire history of First United Church! She shares the same story with the UCW Presbyterial, a regional gathering of United Church women. At the Presbyterial meeting, there are representatives from UCW groups across Ottawa. If anyone is surprised by the lesbian and UCW collaboration, no one says anything. It's not the first time that the word "lesbian" has come up at a UCW gathering.

Sybil Brake, a newcomer to First United in the early '90s, is its new Clerk of Session. She likes the diversity she finds here. "The mix of mainstreams and margins is quite wonderful to behold," she says. She thinks that having the whole issue of sexual orientation discussed and debated and written about was a good thing. "It gave people a chance to reflect on their attitudes and perhaps learn some things that could lead them to change, or at least be open to new possibilities." And change has certainly been the order of the day. The congregation is still growing. Almost half its current membership is new within the past two years. But the old timers haven't left. In fact, the congregation only lost one family in the turbulent Issue years. Stewart, now well into his eighties, still sits every Sunday with his family in the same pew he always has occupied. The liturgy is different now—there's liturgical dance, drama, lots of participation from lay people, young and old, and a lot of laughter—but for him, as for many others who have found a welcome here, this is home!

Maureen O'Neill, a more recent member at First United, thinks that even though the congregation didn't support the 1988 decision of the General Council, that event still had a big impact. "It made it possible to address the issue openly," she says. "It put it on the table. It became something that individual congregations could simply say, 'No, we don't want to deal with this.' We really have changed. I think that it has pushed the boundaries of what it is to be Christian and what it is to be church [by] not only making it more possible for people of differing sexual orientations to be open, but people of differing beliefs, different ways of expressing their faith, to be more open."

D'thea Webster, O'Neill's partner, is a candidate for ministry from Ottawa Presbytery. She recalls when she and O'Neill started attending First United. "They were just in the middle of the discernment process. They were handing out the information packages the first Sunday we were there. When we came back it was the day after that 'day of discernment.' We went into the coffee hour and all of the sheets of paper were up on the wall. I remember saying to myself, 'Yes, I can be comfortable here. I can be me!' It was wonderful."

The congregation's willingness to talk respectfully with one another about difficult issues, combined with the willingness of a few gay and lesbian members to be open about their sexual orientation, sowed the seeds for change at First United. Once the base was established, change happened very rapidly. "I think it became exponential," says Webster. "When we came to First there were really only one or two lesbians who had come out, and a couple of gay men. Within two or three years everything had changed. The space was created by the work done by a few people who came out in that process." One of the early pioneers of change at First United, Bill Siksay, already had a long history of coming out in The United Church of Canada.

8

PREPARING FOR MINISTRY

We ain't where we oughta be, we ain't where we wanna be, and we ain't where we're gonna be, but thank goodness we ain't where we was.

Sojourner Truth

We shall not cease from exploration
 and the end of all our exploring
 will be to arrive where we started
 and know the place for the first time.

T.S. Eliot

South Hill United is a working class congregation in a south Vancouver neighbourhood. Its members don't perceive themselves to be particularly radical. But they have always supported Brian Burke, who was their candidate for ministry. Even a conservative member, who wasn't very supportive of gay rights said, "of course I'd be supportive of our Brian." The day of his ordination, the congregation cancelled its own morning worship and rented a bus to go to the service of celebration. They left Vancouver at 5:30 a.m. in a big bright yellow school bus with the words "South Hill United" emblazoned on the side. After the ordination service they all gathered around the bus for pictures with Brian, the camera capturing their beaming, pride-filled faces. Then they all piled back on the bus, laughing and waving, for the trip back home.

Bill Siksay was raised in The United Church of Canada in Oshawa, Ontario. In 1978, he began theological studies at Vancouver School of Theology, sponsored by an Oshawa congregation that was very proud to have a candidate for the ministry, its first in more than 50 years. At theological school Siksay was open about his sexual orientation. In 1980, he told his family, his minister in his home congregation and the presbytery committee responsible for approving him, that he was gay. The United Church did not yet have any official policy, so no one knew what to do with him. Siksay's file was passed on, like a hot potato, to Bay of Quinte Conference.

Although his congregation continued to support his candidacy, the Conference decided that no lesbian or gay candidate would be approved until the church had an official policy. Siksay remains very active as a lay person in the United Church, but he withdrew his candidacy for ministry. He now runs the constituency office for MP Svend Robinson, Canada's first openly gay member of Parliament. Even today, thoughts of ordination still remain a possibility for Siksay, "but not right now." His partner, Brian Burke, was ordained in 1996.

A little more than a year after Siksay's candidacy was rejected, another Conference found itself considering the same issue with another candidate for ministry, this time a young woman. In 1982, she had completed theological studies and was in the final stages of the process leading to ordination. A few months before she was to be ordained, she told the Hamilton Conference that her marriage was ending, and that she had come to accept herself as a lesbian. Hamilton Conference reacted even more strongly than Bay of Quinte. It passed a resolution saying that it would not ordain or commission to ministry any "self-declared practising" lesbian or gay person. (By "self-declared," they meant that the candidates themselves would have to admit to being homosexual; by "practising" they meant non-celibate.) Hamilton Conference called on the rest of the church to create a similar policy. The lesbian candidate also withdrew. She is now a minister in the Metropolitan Community Church, a denomination with a particular ministry with gay and lesbian people.

In many ways, that is how The Issue really began to heat up in the United Church, with self-declared candidates for ministry identifying themselves, and Conferences asking for a national church policy so they would know what to do with them.

Things did not change overnight in the church. After 1988, even with a policy in place that did not explicitly exclude gays and lesbians, the route to ordination had many roadblocks. Another candidate, "Jim," finished studies for ordination in 1989, a year after the General Council declared that sexual orientation was not, in and of itself, a barrier to ministry. He was due to be settled in Hamilton Conference. The Conference had a church in mind. Although Jim had at no time been public about the fact that he was gay, there were rumours that he and his partner had celebrated a same-gender covenanting service. Before Hamilton Conference could contact the settlement congregation, it received a phone call from someone on the charge saying, "We hear you are planning to settle Jim here. We don't want him." Without settlement, Jim's ordination was on hold. "It was very clear that, because of the action some people took, I could not be ordained," he says.

A year later, in June 1990, Jim was once more presented as a candidate for ordination. By this time, Jim had started a graduate program and applied to be ordained "to further study." This allows candidates who are doing advanced theological studies to be ordained but to defer settlement until they have completed their studies. Amid persistent rumours that he was gay, Jim's name was presented to the Conference annual meeting. Before reaching this point a candidate already has gone through an extensive process of selection interviews at three levels of the church's courts. Usually, Conferences applaud the candidates and approve them for ordination in a routine ballot. In Jim's case, however, people were lined up at the microphones to challenge, and defend, his candidacy. Someone at a microphone said that he was homosexual. The president of Conference stopped him, saying, "We don't do anything on the basis of rumours."

"We have some evidence," yelled someone from the floor. A judicial committee was set up to review the "evidence"—copies of a newsletter from the Community of Concern, a United Church group opposed to ordination of gays and lesbians. Jim's name was mentioned in one of the articles. The judicial committee rejected the evidence but, by now, things were getting nasty. "Well, if you don't believe us, you can just look in their windows," someone called out during the debate. There were groans from the floor of Conference. Finally, Conference simply ran out of time on the agenda. The vote was called and the ballots distributed.

All this time, all the candidates for ordination were seated on a stage at the front of the hall, awaiting their turn. By then, Jim says, he was "a basket case." He went off by himself during the supper break. When he got back, someone said to him quietly, "It's going to be all right." The vote in favour of Jim's ordination was overwhelming. He was ordained the next day. At the end of that year, Jim was given priority for settlement and was placed in a half-time position very close to home. He was there for five years, and by all accounts it was a wonderful experience. He's now at the end of his second year of full-time ministry in another pastoral charge. Though still somewhat closeted, Jim says he has "officially come out to a few people" and they have been very supportive.

❧

Ron Coughlin has seen a lot of changes over the years that he has been a staff person in the national church. In 1988, Coughlin began working in the Division of Ministry Personnel and Education, with responsibility for theological education and ministry vocations, in other words, students and candidates for ordered ministry. His appointment was strongly opposed by some quarters. For about two years, the Division received letters of protest every couple of weeks demanding that he be fired. A series of allegations, all completely unfounded, accused him of embezzling money, molesting children and recruiting only gay and lesbian candidates for ministry. The letters stopped in 1990, when the General Council reaffirmed its 1988 statement concerning sexual orientation and eligibility for ministry.

Coughlin notes that he is now able to get on with his work, unhampered by accusations about his sexual orientation. "In the 10-year period since being hired here, I've seen a lot more acceptance of me as an openly gay person in a national position. There were some Conferences that never invited me to work with them. Now I'm seen simply as a person who does my job." Coughlin also has seen things improving for candidates. "I've found presbyteries much more open and willing to help the process, in being sensitive to who they appoint to a discernment committee so that decisions are made on the basis of suitability, not sexual orientation." The discernment committee is the first level of the approval process for candidates for ordered ministry. Most of the members of the committee come from the candidate's home congregation. While some openly lesbian or gay candidates still find they have to change congregations to be approved, many are finding that the climate is more supportive. The handbook that discernment committees receive explicitly mentions the church's policy on sexual orientation and ministry. According to Coughlin, more and more committees now "take it for granted that they can't discriminate on the basis of sexual orientation. There is a lot more thinking about how to help someone who is lesbian or gay and accept and honour their gifts as part of the church."

Candidates for ordination in the United Church are required to spend eight months in a congregational internship. Coughlin helps oversee the internship program and matches students with placements. When dealing with gay and lesbian students, he recognizes that it's a very short period of time in which to develop sufficient trust for someone to come out. Some people choose to tell their supervisor, but not the whole congregation. Others want the whole congregation to know before they even arrive. Others come out gradually over the eight months.

Because students in internships are being evaluated constantly, the risks are high and the sense of safety low. For some lesbian or gay students, this may be the most difficult part of their training. D'thea Webster consciously made the decision that she was not going to put herself forward as an openly lesbian candidate. As she explains, "I wanted to do ministry and not be identified as 'the lesbian minister.'" She found her internship site a very uncomfortable place to be. It felt very dishonest, she says, and it felt impossible to have her partner, Maureen O'Neill, recognized as part of her family. "It was an extremely conservative and elderly congregation. I wasn't completely closeted. I made it very clear that Maureen was my family. I talked about Maureen and I talked about doing things together. But it was as though Maureen was invisible whenever she was there." Ultimately, Webster decided that the risks of rocking the boat by coming out were too great. If the internship placement fell apart, she could find herself having to wait another year to complete her requirements for ordination. She kept her head down, completed the internship, and vowed that never again would she do ministry in a congregation from within the closet.

At the final stage of the candidacy process, candidates' names are submitted to the transfer committee, a national committee that assigns candidates to a Conference, which later settles them in their first congregational ministry position. Coughlin notes that there have been changes there as well. The transfer committee talks a lot about how to meet the needs of gay and lesbian candidates, whether they are completely open about their orientation or have told the transfer committee in confidence. He says these committees have become better at honouring the candidates' degree of openness, and finding settlement sites where there will be support and acceptance. Since 1988, seven openly lesbian or gay candidates have been settled in pastoral charges. Many others have been open to the transfer committee and have been settled in situations that honour their need to be settled close to their partner, or in settings where they will be able to find personal support.

There also have been changes within theological colleges. Many institutions now have the issue of sexual orientation as an explicit part of their curriculum and policy. At St. Andrew's College, Saskatoon, sexual orientation issues are integrated into the curriculum. When studying theology, students encounter specifically gay and lesbian liberation theology. In pastoral care, they learn how to offer counselling and support to the whole variety of family configurations, sexual orientations and situations that are likely to be present in any congregation. When discussing marriage celebrations, many students also choose to prepare for gay and lesbian covenanting services they may be asked to do once they begin congregational ministry.

St. Andrew's College has had a policy of justice for gays and lesbians since 1992. "We encourage attention and commitment to issues of justice in the church and society with particular concern for the ways individuals and groups are oppressed and marginalized," states the policy. "We are also committed to raising consciousness about the experience in church and society of persons who are gay, lesbian, or bisexual and to eliminating discrimination based on sexual orientation at St. Andrew's College."

Charlotte Caron is co-president of St. Andrew's and professor of pastoral theology. She believes that the policy is a clear indication of change. "To have a policy means there is a commitment to accountability," she says. "If there is a policy, we can call people to account. It's significant because it is structural. If someone is using language that is heterosexist, we can refer back to the policy and say that it's not acceptable." Caron recognizes that no policy can ensure justice. There have to be widespread changes in behaviour and attitudes for that to happen. As she sees it, "there has to be a change of heart for real change to take place. But without appropriate policies, there is rarely significant movement."

Even at colleges that don't have explicit policies, however, there are some signs of ongoing change and openness. At the Atlantic School of Theology in Halifax, students are introduced to issues of sexual orientation as part of their course work in pastoral theology. As one faculty member explains, "the whole life experience of gay and lesbian people has to be raised up. That experience needs to be made more visible so that the straight students can learn how to encounter gay and lesbian people in their pastoral work." Students also come face to face with gay and lesbian experience through their involvement with other students. These days, it would be hard for a student to get through theological college without knowing at least one fellow student who is openly lesbian or gay.

D'thea Webster and her partner, Maureen O'Neill, attended the annual retreat for students, family members and staff at United Theological College, Montreal. O'Neill went to a workshop for partners on what it was like to be a spouse of someone in ministry. It felt good to be treated just the same as everyone else. "I felt very comfortable," she says. The fact that they happened to be a same-gender couple was "simply a non-issue."

The Centre for Christian Studies in Toronto has had a policy of justice for gays and lesbians since the mid-'80s. It states that the centre seeks "to be inclusive of gender, race, sexual orientation and physical ability. We acknowledge that sexuality is a fundamental gift of God and commit ourselves in our program and community life to study, understand and accept that gift." Kay Heuer has been a staff member at the Centre since 1982. She recalls that the policy was relatively easy to establish. "Our hearts and minds were there. Learning is a vulnerable time. One of our commitments is that we would provide space people could trust as safe, for learning to happen." Issues of sexual orientation are definitely considered part of the curriculum.

Corinne Burke is a student at the Centre in what is called the regional program. In this intensive, five-year program, most of her training takes place in her own community, in congregational and outreach settings, and most of her academic work is done by extension. For five weeks every year she attends residential learning programs. She and her female partner live in Kingston, Ontario, with their two children. She feels very much supported at the Centre. "I feel very safe there. The dialogue is on the table. It's not just me raising the issues; they are raising them, too," she says. Burke says her experience as a candidate has been positive so far. "My sexuality hasn't been the primary focus," she says, "but it hasn't been excluded, either." Her student placement at St. Andrew's-By-The-Lake in Kingston also is going well. Burke comes from a Roman Catholic background, where sometimes trying to create change felt to her like "knocking your head against a wall." She sees the United Church as paving the path. "In the United Church the struggle is worth it; you can see the changes," she declares. "The transformation is happening as we speak."

That transformation is going on even in some very unlikely parts of the church. In September 1988 the executive of Maritime Conference declared that in the light of scripture and because of the concerns expressed by presbyteries, pastoral charges and individuals in the Conference, it would only consider as eligible to be received into the ordered ministry or to be settled those whose lifestyle included faithfulness in marriage to a spouse of the opposite sex or celibacy in singleness. Ironically, the Conference did what General Council had been incorrectly accused of doing—limiting the power of congregations to select their own ministers. Although it still has the policy on its books, Bob Campbell, a staff person with Maritime Conference, thinks the Conference may be changing slowly. Through encounters with gay and lesbian people who have come out, some people have changed their opinions. "There is less fear," he says. But, he admits, "it's still a volatile topic for some people."

The Conference settlement committee is responsible for finding settlement sites for candidates who are being ordained. At a meeting in 1997, the question came up about finding congregations willing to accept lesbian or gay ministers. Pastoral relations convenors decided to go back to their presbyteries and begin the process of talking to congregations about which ones might be open to such a possibility. It might seem like a very small step. Campbell thinks it's a significant one, though. It's a sign, he says, "of much greater openness."

In 1997 Hamilton Conference also took a step forward. Fifteen years after it rejected a candidate for ordination because she was a lesbian, another young woman was presented as a candidate who was clearly lesbian. The printed biography that introduced her to the Conference indicated that she was in a relationship with another woman. This fact was made equally clear in her own presentation to the Conference. This time, however, there was no reaction, no outcry or dissent. No one rushed to the microphone to speak against her ordination. People listened attentively and, as with all the other candidates, applauded and cheered heartily when she was finished. No one walked out in protest as she stood, in her rainbow stole, at the ordination service. It was almost as if, well, that's just the way it is now.

9

Settled and Unsettled

Cowardice asks the question: Is it safe? Consensus asks the question: Is it popular? Conscience asks the question: Is it right?

Martin Luther King, Jr.

A United Church minister had started telling a few people in her congregation that she was lesbian. The congregation had decided to consider how it might be more welcoming and supportive of its gay and lesbian members and their families. At its first meeting, she came out to the committee guiding the process. This was news to some members of the committee, but no surprise to one, a man in his seventies. He'd heard rumours about her at Conference at least 10 years earlier. Later he told her how relieved he was that she'd finally said something. "I wanted to let you know I was supportive, but I didn't know if this was something I was supposed to talk about," he said. The next Sunday at coffee hour, the man's wife came up to her minister and gave her a hug and a kiss on the cheek. "I'm just so happy!" she whispered in the minister's ear.

The road to Osage, Saskatchewan, stretches as far as the eye can see beneath an endless sky. Osage is about 100 kilometres south-east of Regina. The prairie here is so flat you can see the next grain elevator 12 kilometres away. Behind the elevators, past the fields of endless blue-green flax, is Osage United Church. Like most of the other buildings in town, the paint is peeling from its white clapboard. On Sunday mornings, at least half the town is in church. Hazel Glover plays the piano here. She's good at finding tunes people know. They say that as long as she plays, there will still be church at Osage.

Glover can see most of the town from her kitchen window, where she sits with the newspaper spread out in front of her, the Saturday crossword almost completed. Now in her mid-80s, Glover has lived in Osage for more than 75 years. When asked about the size of the community, she pauses to count. Someone died, someone had a baby, a couple moved away. There are 21 people now, she concludes. Osage is the smallest church on the three-point pastoral charge of Prairie Points. The charge was formed in 1996, as an amalgamation of churches at Fillmore, Osage and Creelman. It's what's known as a "settlement charge." It's too small and remote to attract ministers by call. Mostly, its clergy are settled here in their first church placement. The most recent minister is the Rev. Brian Burke. The congregation knew, before Burke arrived, that he was openly gay.

When asked if this is a concern at all, Glover shakes her head. "It didn't disturb the community at all. A few people let it bother them a bit at first, but it isn't really an issue. Not for most of us." There isn't much more to say. Glover likes her minister. She thinks he's a good preacher and good at pastoral care. Talk soon turns to other things, the need for rain, her son's new tow truck, her newest great-grandson.

Burke was raised a Catholic. In 1979, he met Bill Siksay, who was at that time a candidate for ordination in the United Church. Burke says Siksay was "one of those pioneers who paid a price for being the first in line." When their relationship began, Burke and Siksay looked for a United Church home where they could feel welcome as a couple. They found it at South Hill United in Vancouver, and later at First United Church, Ottawa. In 1988, they attended General Council together. Sitting in the visitors gallery, listening to the debate about who would or would not be considered eligible for ordered ministry, Burke first began to consider ordination himself.

Burke's first interview was with a committee from the board at South Hill. Because the congregation knew Burke and Siksay as a couple, Burke's sexual orientation was clear from the beginning and wasn't an issue. He was completely open about his sexual orientation throughout the entire candidacy process, including settlement.

Elaine Driver was born and raised in rural Saskatchewan. As a young woman, she moved to Fillmore to teach school, and ended up marrying a local farmer. She can't remember having ever had a problem with homosexuality. "I have always believed it's just the way you are," she explains.

Driver remembers being at Saskatchewan Conference when the debate first started in the United Church. "There were some real dinosaurs up there ranting and raving, with all sorts of stupid notions about what homosexuality is." Driver doesn't mince words.

She also knows how it is in small towns. People know everyone and everything that happens, and the minister lives in a fish-bowl. She recalls a time when a previous minister, who was single, had someone visiting from out of town. "One of the neighbours was very frustrated. She phoned me to ask who was visiting, complaining that, even standing on her toilet seat, she couldn't see where the license plate was from."

Shortly after the Prairie Points charge was formed Driver was disappointed to discover that the minister at Creelman was leaving. Someone at Creelman said, "We've had three women in a row, it's time we had a man." Driver recalls blurting out to a friend, in some frustration, "Well, I sure hope they get their man, and I hope he's gay!" The friend called back a few months later with the news. "Well, they got their man, and guess what...!"

Driver is solidly behind Burke and his ministry at Prairie Points. "The fact that he is so gifted in ministry work makes it hard for people to say anything bad about him," she says with fondness. "It's the type of person he is and the type of work he does. I once said to Brian, 'God sent you here to help people understand a bit better about homosexuals.' And God knows there's still a lot of understanding to be created."

Dale Wiggins, another Saskatchewan farmer, has been United Church since the '50s. Like most United Church people, he was part of all the discussion about The Issue. In 1988, he chaired Saskatchewan Conference. "I knew where I was at. I don't think the debate changed my mind that much," he says. "Why should we hinder people because they're different?" He did have some initial reservations, however, about Burke being settled at Prairie Points. His main concern was that it was such a newly created charge. "I felt people were already looking for an excuse to say it wouldn't work, being a brand new pastoral charge; we were starting brand new with Brian. We had no previous experience to fall back on."

Wiggins feels most people have accepted their gay minister reasonably well. "Two or three people more or less forgot to come to church since he's been here, but he has generally been well received." It just doesn't seem to be an issue, not for this congregation, not right now. As far as Dale is concerned, Brian's acceptance has a lot to do with who Brian is. It was a new issue for some people, but now people wouldn't hesitate to say yes to another gay or lesbian minister. "He's a great person to have around!" And as for the people who forgot to come to church, the ladies are talking with them at the weekly quilting bee. They'll probably come back in time.

❧

Things did not go nearly so smoothly the first time the United Church tried to find a congregation willing to have a gay man settled as its minister. On May 24, 1992, Tim Stevenson became the first openly gay man ordained by The United Church of Canada. According to United Church policy, someone can be ordained or commissioned only if "there is assurance of transfer and settlement." In Stevenson's case, however, settlement didn't happen until nearly a year later, in 1993. When he was ordained, the settlement committee of Manitoba and Northwestern Ontario Conference felt confident it could find a congregation willing to receive him. British Columbia Conference took Manitoba at its word and ordained him. A little pastoral charge in southwestern Manitoba agreed to something no other charge in the country had done—to consider the possibility of having a gay man as their minister.

Stevenson likens the process of breaking new ground to the United Church's experience of ordaining women. "Until Lydia E. Gruchy was ordained in Saskatchewan in 1936, people thought it was impossible. It was still tough for women afterwards, but at least someone had been ordained. The problem I was running up against was that no one had ever done this before. People were shocked, and they thought it couldn't be done." Some from the Hartney-Lauder-Dand Pastoral Charge thought it just might be possible, and they were willing to give it a try.

The only sounds around the Dand church are those of birds and prairie wind. The church's fresh-cut lawns border rolling fields of soft blue and brilliant yellow. A yellow bird the colour of canola alights on a nearby branch. Inside the small, simple sanctuary a banner proclaims, "New life!" The church has been here since the 1880s when the nearby town of Deloraine was established. Originally it was Quaker. The building passed into United Church hands in the 1930s. Dand is the smallest point on the charge—about 21 families attend regularly. It's a family-oriented place, with strong community links. People see each other at the grocery and hardware store. Their families are intertwined, their lives interconnected. Just now, some of them are gathering in the coffee shop in Deloraine. The Wiggins, the Days and a few others from town sip coffee from white porcelain mugs. Five years later, as they talk about their failed attempt to have Tim Stevenson come and be their minister, there is still a deep sense of disappointment. There are still tears.

In 1992 the pastoral relations committee at Hartney-Lauder-Dand had encountered trouble finding a minister to fill its vacancy. Committee members decided they would go the settlement route. When Stevenson was presented as a possibility, the committee was very impressed by the skills and experience he had to offer. They considered the prospect very seriously. They introduced him to each of the three congregations on the pastoral charge. At each meeting, members were told that Stevenson was gay, and had a chance to meet him. In each case, the response was polite. Next, the committee circulated a questionnaire to all members and adherents, along with an information sheet on Stevenson and on the settlement process. Finally, after several more congregational meetings, the committee met to make its decision. The committee members strongly supported Stevenson. Sadly, based on the responses from members and adherents, they were forced to conclude that the pastoral charge was not yet ready to have a gay minister. Their meeting ended with praying, crying and more praying.

Claire Day lives on a farm just north of Deloraine. Some of their land borders the Dand church. A nurse by profession, she worked for 16 years in the seniors home. The Days raised hogs for 29 years and canola. Initially, Day was angry that the pastoral charge had turned down Stevenson. Lately, she has become a little more reconciled. "You can only be responsible for yourself, not what anyone else says or thinks," she explains. "That kind of freed me from my anger." She's starting to see that some good did come out of it. "The issue opened up people's eyes. They began talking about things they didn't ever want to think about. We had a friend who was very homophobic who was on the pastoral relations committee. He met Tim and began to see the person rather than the sexual orientation. He did a complete turnaround."

Most people in the charge didn't want to talk about the sexual orientation issue when it was first raised in the United Church, but not many people left. In 1988 the charge lost only two families—one over The Issue and one because someone did a liturgical dance in church. The process of meeting Stevenson and the discussion that ensued did at least begin to open up the conversation.

Cathey Day, Claire's 30-year-old daughter, jumps into the conversation. "It was a great opportunity to educate people in the community," she declares. Cathey was at the United Church Youth Forum at the General Council in Morden, Manitoba, in 1984. She learned about the sexual orientation issue there and became convinced that it was a justice issue. "Why did we care?" she asks. "Because it's a human rights issue. Whether we live in rural Manitoba or downtown Toronto, we all have minds and question things."

The passion in her voice is undiminished. "What gets more to our core than human rights issues?" Certainly, the issue touched a nerve in the whole community. "The coffee shop talk was very hot. Everyone knew what everyone else thought," she declares.

Shirley Brown continues where Cathey leaves off. "For me, it's about the very basics of Christianity and being the church," she says, wiping away tears. "If he had lied and said he wasn't gay, he'd have had the job. The church is supposed to be about honesty and truthfulness. He told the truth and he didn't get in!" She admits she's still pretty angry.

Marg Franklin grew up in Winnipeg, and married a farmer in Hartney. "We're really only playing at farming," her husband, Glen, chips in. "There's no money in it." They both have a strong United Church connection. Marg served on national church committees and as chair of presbytery. She was a commissioner to General Council in 1988, and recalls how she felt after the final vote. "I just went back to my room shaking my head and wondering where we were going." But The Issue didn't go away. It made her stop and think, and begin to discover what she really felt. She says one of the defining moments was when she suddenly asked herself, "What if one of your kids turns out to be gay?" She finally concluded that sexuality is a gift. "To deny the whole church this gift is so sad," she says, "because we're losing so much." Many people at Dand feel they lost a whole lot by not having Stevenson come and be their minister. Although they appreciate their current minister, they still look back on 1992 as an opportunity lost.

In most congregations, even ones willing to accept a lesbian or gay minister, homosexuality would still be considered a liability. There is one congregation, however, where it's considered an asset. The Church of the Deaf in Winnipeg was founded in 1919 by deaf people in the community. Worship services are informal and inclusive. There isn't much singing, but there's lots of dialogue. Sermons aren't preached, they're discussed or dramatized, and the whole community gets involved in the conversation. The church meets in a local community centre. Members sit in a circle of chairs. Since sign language is the way they communicate, it's essential they see one another.

Speaking through a sign language interpreter, members of the congregation talk about a decision they made two years ago to receive an openly gay man as their minister. In 1994, Ken DeLisle was coming up for settlement in Manitoba. He and his partner had been in a committed relationship for

15 years. After their previous experience with Stevenson, the settlement committee recognized the need to consult carefully with whichever congregation was receiving him. The Church of the Deaf was approached. The congregation was told about DeLisle's gifts and interests in ministry and they were told that he was openly gay. Church members were invited to take the time they needed to consider the issues and decide if they wanted DeLisle to be their minister.

It didn't take them long to make up their minds. As they explained, the choice was an easy one. DeLisle had the gifts and skills for ministry that they needed and wanted and, in addition, he had two other assets. As a gay man, he knew what it was like to be part of an invisible minority. He knew, just as deaf people did, what it was like to be marginalized and sometimes excluded. Furthermore, he'd know how to be an advocate. As long-time member Mar Koskie explains it, "it meant he would understand us better." He sees many parallels between the experiences of deaf and homosexual people, since "both experience oppression." DeLisle is well liked in the community, according to Mar Koskie. "He is very respectful of our culture." It is time, he says, to stop saying someone can't do something just because they're gay. Or deaf.

For Ken Anderson, another long-time member at the Church of the Deaf, the issues are equally simple. "I believe Ken was called by God to become a pastor of our church. I respect that call from God. I think the Bible says not to judge other people. So I don't." DeLisle says that, for him, this was the first time he'd ever had that dimension of who he is—his sexual orientation—valued as something positive. It took a community of deaf people, a community used to being marginalized, to recognize and even celebrate that gift.

As for Stevenson, after his year-long wait, he found several congregations willing to welcome him and his gifts for ministry. In May 1993, he was settled back in British Columbia in St. Paul's United Church, Burnaby. Stevenson was well-known to the congregation; in 1991, he had served a four-month internship there. He was delighted to be back. They were thrilled to have him. And when he was elected to the provincial legislature in 1996, the congregation went on to call another openly gay minister, the Rev. Philip Cable.

10

I Never Thought I'd See the Day

History, although sometimes made up of the few acts of the great, is more often shaped by the many acts of the small.

Mark Yost

To be nobody but yourself—in a world which is doing its best, night and day, to make you everybody else—means to fight the hardest battle which any human being can fight, and never stop fighting.

e.e. cummings

First-St. Andrew's United in London, Ontario, has been quietly welcoming gay and lesbian people as members for a number of years. In the summer of 1997, someone suggested doing something around Gay Pride Day. They proposed a Sunday worship service that explicitly welcomed gay and lesbian people. There was a bit of a mix-up in the publicity—the service got announced in all the London media as the first event in Gay Pride week. That wasn't the intent, but the congregation wasn't particularly perturbed. These things happen. It turned out to be a blessed occasion. A number of gay and lesbian people from the community attended. Several gay and lesbian members of the congregation participated in the service. Everyone went outside for lemonade afterwards. It may just become a regular event. There are some congregations who have lost members over The Issue, but that day, First-St. Andrew's gained a few.

❧

Philip Cable grew up in Cobourg, Ontario. He and his family were very active at Trinity United Church. The journey from Trinity to St. Paul's in Burnaby, British Columbia, is a long one. Cable is now divorced, after a marriage that lasted almost 17 years, and has two children. He began the coming out process during his final year at seminary. He says the first opening of the closet door was "sort of a sense that this is an interesting thing to learn about myself but I'm happily married. I shared that information with my former wife, and we both agreed that life was great, why should anything change?" He was ordained in May 1988 in Bay of Quinte Conference. He was really rattled by the ordination debate because of what he knew deep inside, but he says, "I was really naïve as to what the repercussions would be for me and for my family."

After ordination, Cable was settled in a five-point pastoral charge in the Maritimes. Then the summer of 1988 hit. "It would be safe to say that's a very conservative area," Cable says. "People I was serving were pretty distraught about the Victoria decision. I can't tell you how thrilled they were to have a married man in the manse and tricycles in the driveway. They had no idea what this was doing to me. They would ask my opinion and I would say, my job is not to state my opinions but to make sure you feel heard." In the meantime, however, Cable himself was feeling horribly silenced. "After a year and a half of that I realized I was just kicking myself. It was a long, difficult, hard process to come to terms with accepting my gay self and the rightness of expressing that. Thankfully my relationship was and still is a friendship based on openness and honesty. Although it was a painful process for both of us to come to terms with the need for separation it was something that we worked out over a long period of time."

Cable decided to leave ministry when he began to recognize his need to come out. "I knew I couldn't do it in that setting," he says. "I handed in my resignation and I was encouraged by colleagues to seek a call somewhere else." He found a church closer to support networks and a larger visible gay community. "During that year I burned out trying to be super dad, super minister, super husband and also trying to figure out who am I and what this gay component means," he recalls.

He eventually decided to leave the congregational setting and move into hospital chaplaincy, which he did for the next six years. He realized he was not doing what he really felt called to do, but didn't think congregational ministry would ever again be an option. "When I left pastoral ministry I assumed that I would never be able to serve a pastoral charge again," Cable says. "I couldn't serve a church if I couldn't be out and if I couldn't speak freely. The first surprise was hearing myself say, 'I think I want to start looking.'"

He applied to a number of churches across the country and received lots of rejection letters. When he applied to St. Paul's United in Burnaby, he was open about his sexual orientation. "They wouldn't have asked me, but they were open to hearing that part of my story," he says. "The people on the search committee were very excited about having me come. This is a supportive community who have done homework and follow through with actions."

Cable is very happy in his ministry in his new congregation. It is important for him to be able to be open about who he is, including his sexual orientation. "When I'm seen, I blossom," he says. "And when I blossom people celebrate me being around and I feel more accepted and affirmed and freer to blossom some more."

Former moderator Marion Best uses the same image when she speaks of gay and lesbian people being open in the church. "Always it's the story of gay and lesbian people who have blossomed when they could be open and honest about themselves," she says. "It's not gospel to ask people to hide part of who they are. There are congregations that aren't getting the very best of what a person could offer because they aren't out. It comes full circle when the community says we want you and all of your gifts and we want you for who you are." Every so often, it seems, there are congregations that say just that.

It's a Saturday morning in the spring of 1993. The pastoral relations committee of Whitehorse United Church is talking with a prospective new minister, the Rev. Rob Oliphant. There was a telephone interview a few weeks earlier. Everyone liked what they'd heard, so they invited Oliphant to come up to Whitehorse for a weekend interview. Oliphant had already told the chair of the committee that he was gay. The previous night he informed the whole group, telling them toward the end of the evening so people could go away and think about it. Now, as the group reconvenes, the chair invites people to say how they're feeling.

For three members of the committee, Oliphant's sexual orientation is a non-issue. For others, it's something about which they need to talk. One woman admits she was shocked. "I went home last night and said to myself, 'I'd better have a bath.' I sat in the tub, with a glass of Dubonnet and thought 'My adult children would have no difficulty with this. Why am I? It's time for me to move.'"

Another man started to cry. "I never thought I'd want one of you to be my minister," he says with some feeling, "Now, I don't know why, but I do." From that moment on, Oliphant had no doubt that here in this place he had found a call to ministry. The committee decided to invite Oliphant to be the congregation's new minister. Oliphant moved in July. His partner Marco joined him in October.

Whitehorse United isn't the first place you'd imagine calling an openly gay man as its minister. It's in a town of less than 20,000 people, nearly 3,000 kilometres north of Vancouver in the Yukon. The town is conservative, a place where politics are polarized. The church itself is a traditional one. In 1988 in reaction to the General Council decision, the congregation passed a motion stating that it would never call a homosexual minister. They'd had many years of traditional ministry with a conservative theological bent, but one that included a message of love and compassion. The church disagreed with the 1988 decision, but never lost its commitment to the wider church. Its givings to the Mission and Service Fund didn't decline after 1988, they went up.

Over the course of his first two years at Whitehorse United, Oliphant gradually came out to the congregation. Now his sexual orientation is a non-issue. He and his partner are well accepted in the church community, and Oliphant is happy in his ministry. After more than 13 years of congregational ministry, he considers it "the easiest place I've ever been to be a minister."

The decision of Whitehorse United to call a gay minister came as a surprise to some. The bigger surprise is that it's not the only congregation to have done so. Currently there are 27 openly gay or lesbian clergy serving United Church congregations. In 1988, there wasn't one congregation with an openly homosexual minister. Most people thought it would be a long time before there ever would be. Former moderator the Very Rev. Rev. Bob Smith puts it this way, "I'm not suggesting we have emerged into sunlit pastures, but I wouldn't ever have believed we would have come this far this fast."

Smith went through his own conversion around The Issue in the early '80s. The turning point was a time he agreed to fill in at the last minute for someone who'd agreed to preach at Metropolitan Community Church, a denomination whose ministry is primarily with gay and lesbian people and their friends. Smith had never before been to a gathering of openly gay people. There, he met the 18-year-old son of a close family friend, a boy he'd known all his life. The young man came up to Smith and said, "Mom told me to tell you that she knows, and it's OK." For Smith, this was what he calls "a life-changing experience. I was being prepared for something."

Shaughnessy Heights United Church in Vancouver may well have been that "something." Shaughnessy Heights is what some people call an establishment church—large, prosperous, multi-staffed, in an upper-class neighbourhood. At one count, it had 128 doctors on its congregational list. Smith was a minister there for a little more than 10 years, beginning in 1982. In September 1983, just shortly after Smith had arrived, the board received a request from Affirm (a United Church gay and lesbian organization) to hold a monthly service in the chapel. The board approved the request but, subsequently, 12 members of the congregation called for a congregational meeting to oppose the board's action.

Ward Allen remembers those days, along with most of the rest of the congregation's history. Allen has been at Shaughnessy Heights for more than 75 years. He remembers the days when he and other youngsters went all around the community selling red cardboard bricks, three for a quarter, to help pay for a church building. And he remembers the time Shaughnessy Heights started to buzz about the issue of homosexuality, the time when, in his words, "all hell broke loose."

Back then, Allen says, he had his own prejudices about homosexuals. He certainly didn't want a group of them meeting in the church building. He went to talk to his family doctor about it, and somehow in the course of that conversation changed his mind completely. But he knows there are still "many other Ward Allens in the church community."

In 1984, in what Smith describes as "the ugliest meeting I've ever been at in my life," the board's decision was overturned by a narrow margin. The congregation refused to let Affirm use its chapel for worship. "Then they set out to get me," says Smith, "and I would have had to resign except that I went away to General Council. And I came back as Moderator of the United Church." This, says Smith, "is the background for the most astonishing transformation I've ever seen."

Over the next few years, Smith and others in the congregation began to visit families who had withdrawn their support after the United Church's decision in 1988. Some people came back into the church, but were quite clear that "if you ever call one of them as a minister, I'm leaving."

Ryerson United Church, Shaughnessy Heights' closest United Church neighbour, is also an establishment congregation, in the same lawns-and-hedges neighbourhood. In 1993, Ryerson called the Rev. Gary Paterson, an openly gay man, to be its minister. When Smith heard this, he commented,

"I can't believe I would live long enough to see the day Ryerson would do this. I know I'll never live long enough to see it happen at Shaughnessy."

Paterson's roots run deep in Vancouver soil. His great-grandparents cleared land there 120 years ago. He also has deep United Church roots. He grew up in the church, was involved in church youth programs and had what he calls "a typical teen break from the church" before experiencing a call to ministry. He was ordained in 1977.

Like many others, Paterson left congregational ministry for a time when he started to come to terms with his sexual orientation. In 1982, he started working with the United Church's British Columbia Conference. At that point, he was living in what he calls a "glass closet." His partner, Tim Stevenson, came to staff parties and was welcomed there. People knew, but didn't talk about it. "I never lied, but I never made any public statement, either," he says with a smile. In 1989, Paterson returned to ministry in a congregation, this time at First United Church, in Vancouver's lower east side. There, in an inner-city congregation with a strong social justice focus and an intentional outreach ministry to the marginalized, Paterson became much more public about his sexual orientation. He was surprised to discover that some people still did not know. "One person I told about Tim and me said, 'Oh, that's good news to hear. I kept wondering. You're such a nice person and I didn't want you to be lonely!'"

When Paterson received an letter of invitation from Ryerson United Church asking him to consider applying for a vacancy there, he was quite taken aback. "I thought of them as more conservative, more typically United Church, than First United. I assumed that most of them would know I was gay and that would rule me out as a viable candidate." Paterson made sure that both the committee and the congregation knew he was gay before there was a vote on the call. There was discussion at the congregational meeting, but it wasn't particularly heated. The vote passed easily. When Paterson was introduced to the congregation a few months later, he was greeted with wild applause. "I really felt I'd made the right decision," he recalls. "I could feel the bond between minister and congregation starting to form." Four years later, Paterson is still very much "in love" with the Ryerson United Church community. "It's a great congregation. It's delightful to be here!" he says emphatically.

There were some people who were upset by the decision. Out of the 500 members, about 20 left. There were a number of others who indicated that they might leave, but most of these people, once they came to know Paterson personally, decided to stay. In 1997, a group of people from Ryerson

United decided to walk in Vancouver's Gay Pride parade. Gay and straight, ranging in age from three to 70, they carried a banner that proudly proclaimed "Ryerson United Church: A Caring, Inclusive, and Diverse Christian Community." What Smith and others thought would never happen in their lifetime had happened at Ryerson United Church.

Then, from down the street at Shaughnessy Heights, came even more astounding news. In the spring of 1994, almost exactly 10 years after the congregation refused to let a group of gay and lesbian Christians worship in its chapel, Shaughnessy Heights United Church called Sally Harris as one of its ordained ministers. They called her knowing that she was in loving and committed relationship with another woman. A lot can happen in 10 years.

11

THE GLASS CLOSET

Life only demands from the strength you possess. Only one feat is possible—not to have run away.

Dag Hammarskjold

"During the heating season, board meetings were held in the manse so they didn't have to heat up the church. 'Peter' and I had a romantic dinner that night, and there we were, with our arms around each. Suddenly, we heard this clearing of the throat. I looked up, and there in the archway of the dining room stood this prominent parishioner. He had walked in, thinking the board meeting was that night. He hadn't rung, because they don't. Maybe he knocked and we didn't hear. Peter scampered up the stairs like a scared rabbit.

"I was left standing there talking to 'Fred.' I quickly resolved the misunderstanding, that there was no board meeting. He said nothing about what he'd just witnessed. I didn't sleep a wink all night, tossing and turning. I imagined the worst, that it was all over. Fred was this crusty old man, very devoted to the church, opinionated, opinions slightly to the right of Atilla the Hun, quite intimidating; that was all the Fred I knew. I kept waiting for the other shoe to fall. Sunday came, and I preached without looking at him. He was in church, nothing said, he was just his regular grumpy self. Weeks and months passed and finally I decided maybe he didn't see as much as I thought he did. He never said anything.

"A year or so later, Fred was dying of cancer. I had become very fond of his wife, although I was still scared of Fred. One day he was released to die at home, and I went up to see him in his bedroom. On his deathbed, in his own inimitable way, he says, to me, wheezing through his oxygen mask, 'You're queer aren't you?'

"'Yeah, you've known for a long time haven't you?'

"'Yeah.'

"'So how does that sit with you?'

"'At this point in time I've got more important things to worry about.'

"'Yes, I guess you do.'

"And then he said, 'Rob is queer, my son. And I never treated him very well and I feel bad about that.'

"Three days later he died, and we buried him. It was true, he had this gay son, Rob. I was able to tell Rob that these words were said to me but they were really intended for him, but Fred just couldn't seem to find a way to tell him. This time Fred had a chance to get it right, and he did respect me. I think it was his way of rectifying what had gone wrong with Rob."

As long as the United Church has existed, there have been gay clergy. Often, they have lived in fear of being discovered and forced to leave. Sometimes, a few people may have known or suspected, but nothing was ever said. Keeping the secret can have a high personal cost.

The 1988 decision of the United Church didn't mean that suddenly most gay and lesbian clergy felt safe to identify themselves. One gay man left General Council in 1988 saying to friends that he was going home to build a bigger and more secure closet, because now people in the community would be scrutinizing his every move. In many places, there was such a tremendous outpouring of anger and outrage that gay and lesbian clergy felt, if anything, even less safe.

The Rev. Lynette Miller has worked for many years in different levels of the church. She recalls a time shortly after 1988 when she was working in the Winnipeg Presbytery office. "I had a friend who went as a presbytery representative to a congregation whose minister was gay and very deeply closeted." The presbytery representative knew this, though of course the congregation didn't, Miller recalls. "At the meeting members of the congregation were asking questions like 'So you're telling me that the United Church is going to force us to accept a homosexual minister?' The presbytery representative was able to arrange his face in perfect control and say, 'No, it's quite simple. If you don't want to have a homosexual minister you don't have to call one.' [He said this] knowing that their gay minister was sitting right there beside them."

There are signs of gradual change—a lessening of fear, a greater comfort with having some people know, but the reality is still that, in spite of a relatively inclusive church policy, most of the lesbian or gay clergy in The United Church of Canada are not public about their sexual orientation. Many live in what has been called a "glass closet"—some people know, sometimes most people know, but everyone looks the other way. Nothing is said.

"Tom" is quite comfortable to leave things that way. He is a minister in a mid-sized urban congregation. Tom lives with his male partner in a house they bought together several years ago. He doesn't go out of his way to hide his relationship. In fact, he assumes that anyone in the congregation who wants to know probably does know. But nothing is ever said. Tom thinks this congregation is like a lot of families, including his own, families that know at some level about a lesbian or gay family member, but really don't want to talk about it. Tom has only told one of his siblings.

"My partner and I are very much a couple. We go to all the family functions, on both sides. That's sort of a given, but we don't talk about it," he says. Families are like that in the rural community where Tom was raised. People get uncomfortable if things get named. "My family dealt with my sexual orientation by knowing who I was and just coming to know me and my partner as normal people," he explains.

Tom figures it is much the same for the congregation. "If they'd been forced to talk about it, that would have been very foreign. But it was put on the table gently and they were allowed to nibble at it in their own way. They could come to accept it in their own time." Tom never gets questions from the congregation about his marital status. He doesn't have to deal with hints or suggestions. "That's the way my family deals with things. 'We know, let's just not talk about it.' But in a positive way—it's not that they're pretending something else is the reality. It's more like they're saying, 'This is life, this is you, let's get on with it.'"

Barbara Rumscheidt teaches part time at the Atlantic School of Theology in Halifax. She has been studying the United Church's response to sexual orientation and ministry for a long time. She did a master's thesis on the topic. She also has been an advocate of gay rights issues for many years as a member of PFLAG (Parents and Friends of Lesbians and Gays) and Lesbian and Gay Rights of Nova Scotia, a group that worked to get sexual orientation included as prohibited grounds of discrimination in the provincial human rights legislation. Rumscheidt thinks the issue of sexual orientation and ministry is still very much unresolved, at least in the Maritimes. "There is a kind of silence which is very much like the silence of avoidance. There is certainly a prevailing taboo. Just don't mention the whole thing. Forget it, move on. It's gone underground," she says, noting that there are still very few people who are out.

Across the United Church, most of the 27 openly lesbian or gay clergy serving congregations are in urban centres. Bob Smith believes that some change is happening, but very gradually. "The ratio between those who say it's as bad as it always was and those who are saying it's not as bad has changed," he says. "I'm not denying the reality or the suffering. Most of the lesbians I know in ministry are closeted. I know only slightly more gay men who are open. The fact that they're closeted says they don't think it's safe."

"Suzanne" is an ordained minister in what she considers to be a very liberal congregation in a suburban setting. People in the congregation studied the issue in the past, and consider themselves to be fairly open and tolerant. Theirs was one of the few congregations to put forward a resolution in 1988 that supported the inclusion of lesbians and gays in ministry. Although she has been here a few years, Suzanne hasn't felt comfortable letting the congregation know her lesbian identity. She has told two people directly and figures that maybe another 10 per cent of the congregation either know or assume, but as for the rest, she's not sure. "There are a few people who would be quite comfortable," she says tentatively, "but I think most wouldn't be." The fear of coming out or being found out is less now than it was, Suzanne says, certainly compared to her time spent in a rural, multi-point ministry in the '80s. But there is still a degree of caution.

Suzanne sometimes finds it hard not to be able to share more of her personal life in the congregation. "When I preach, it would sometimes be nice to mention things that relate to my partner or my home life, but I can't. I'm still very much aware of the silence, and my patience around that gets less and less." One big concern is the impact of coming out if she ever decided to seek a call in another congregation. Unless she wants this to be the last place she serves, she thinks she'd be crazy to come out. Let's face it, there just aren't that many churches willing to call an out lesbian.

It's a real fear. Word does get around, and sometimes calls are lost because of it. One minister, "Patrick," tells of losing a call in 1992 because the congregation found out he was gay. He had been through several interviews, members of the joint pastoral relations committee had come to hear him preach. Patrick had not disclosed his sexual orientation. There had been some veiled questions in the interview such as "Are you a family man?" which he sidestepped. "Personally I think it's political suicide to openly declare oneself," he says. They had worked out all the details of the call. On the floor of the congregational meeting, however, one person stood up and announced that their potential new minister was gay. The information had been passed on from his home town, in another province. The call was defeated by two votes—52 in favour, 54 against.

"That was the most damaging thing that has ever happened to me, professionally and psychologically," Patrick says. "I had been around the hatred and the animosity of the church courts. It took me some time to recover." He believes that because of "the pain and anguish that is inflicted," he has grown spiritually. "I used to struggle with being normal. And now I'm just content to be very, very different. There has been a deepening within me. I'm able to go to some pool of mirth and drink from it, content to be a living, vibrant human being that has lots of gifts that don't hinge on being gay. We're human beings."

Some people, and some congregations, are able to accept ministers who are gay and lesbian. There is often sadness that the "glass closet" creates such a barrier. They would like to support closeted lesbian or gay clergy, but don't feel they can say anything. In many cases, the whole community may know, but nothing ever gets said. "Naomi," a young woman from a small rural community, remembers two single women, clergy from neighbouring charges, who met and formed a relationship. Apparently the whole town talked about it, although the two clergy thought it was a complete secret. Naomi had a very close relationship with one of the women, her own minister. "I really liked her. She was so funny, so neat. She had a huge influence on me as a young person." At first, Naomi didn't want to believe the rumours that her minister was a lesbian. "I didn't care, I still liked her." Naomi has stayed in contact with her former minister, but nothing has ever been said between them about sexual orientation. "Now, I'm just sad that she never told me. I wanted her to know that I accepted her and loved her no matter what her sexual orientation," she says.

But Naomi knows there are others in the community who would not have been so supportive. She doubts the minister would have been able to stay if she had been openly lesbian. "Others in the community can enjoy and appreciate the person and all their gifts, but don't want to know about it. The whole community can know, but as long as it's not stated, they'll carry on as usual." That's not the case, however, if sexual orientation is made explicit. "There would have been enough people asking her to leave," says Naomi. "Even now, 10 years later, people still say to my mother, 'Aren't you worried that your daughter is such good friends with her?'"

The reality of coming out, as gay and lesbian people know, is that you can never predict the consequences. Sometimes the people that one least expects to be supportive are, and sometimes when things look fine, the consequences can be devastating. The stakes are high: the potential loss of family, friends, job, home. Even personal safety may be a factor.

One United Church staff person talks about what she calls "the Friday evening from hell!" It was winter 1997, at a meeting with a pastoral charge and its clergy. Members of the charge had recently found out that their minister and partner had held a celebration of their commitment. The couple was living in the manse. The minister had been in the congregation for several years. At the meeting, things broke down very quickly. "We heard all sorts of vitriolic stuff," said the staff person. "It was pretty horrible, the anger, the hatred." The presbytery people there that night decided that, for the safety of the couple and their family, they would immediately remove them from ministry there, and from the community. "I said I would hold the congregational people there personally responsible for letting the community know that they were expected to be safe, that their cars in the driveway would be safe, that their belongings would be safe. It's one of the few times I've ever made such a statement." The minister, who had already accepted a call to another church when this happened, left a month early, with pay.

One lesbian clergy person, who also lives in a glass closet, thinks the United Church has moved to a point of tolerance, but not acceptance. "As long as it's not named, from the pulpit, in the media, we just turn a blind eye," she says. "In most cases it's not something that's celebrated, but it's tolerable." But there are still places one can't even count on people to be tolerant.

12

LIFE TOGETHER

And every heart its doubts or dangers past
Beats on its way for love and home at last.

John Clare

"There was a rural community in our Conference in which a woman in ministry settled. Her partner, who was less than an hour away, was losing her place to live, and had also lost a job. They decided they would live together in the manse. I kept saying 'Don't do that! Do you realize the risk you are putting yourself in?' They decided they were going to go ahead and take that chance, and it worked beautifully. She has lived there for three years. It worked just fine. I don't think there was anyone in that whole rural community who didn't understand the relationship. I think they chose not to. There is a lot of selective blindness, particularly if you love the minister.

"If she were to leave, I think they would be open to anyone. It has created more space for the next person. Had they come together and moved in where the minister was not known, I'm not sure what would have happened. But she had been there awhile and had done some really good funerals. She had been with people, was known and cared for and loved, and she used a lot of integrity. It is now a much different place than it was then. It would be one of those places where we'd say, when it comes to settlement, that would be an OK place for a lesbian or gay person."

❧

That same scenario, with minor variations, has repeated itself many times in the United Church. Since 1988, there is more consciousness of what it might mean for two women to live together in the manse. Sometimes congregations tolerate it, sometimes they accept it, sometimes all hell breaks loose. One of the problems is that there is virtually no way to "test the waters," no way to know if a congregation or community is likely to be a safe place or not.

"Marion" moved into a congregation to be near her partner, Jane, who worked in a nearby town. "It was a move that allowed us to be as close as possible," said Marion, "but our hope was that we would live together. We often talked about how this could happen." When Jane lost her job, Marion approached the congregation to ask permission for Jane to move into the manse. Legally, this isn't required, since the manse is considered the minister's private residence, but they decided this would be a courtesy to the congregation. The reasons Marion gave were the job loss, financial benefits, security and companionship. The board said, "Yes, it's your house and you have the right to decide who lives there."

Before the move happened, a minister from a nearby town phoned the chair of the board to say that the women were in a lesbian relationship. Rumours started flying. Several key families in the congregation threatened to withdraw financial support. The chair, while supportive, advised against the move. For Jane, there was a real sense of betrayal and hurt, "that one of our colleagues in ministry had done this." Marion says, "I felt deep rage." But both women also felt a lot of sadness. As Jane expresses it, "It felt like things had not progressed much in the 14 years I've been associated with the church. The relationship I once had with the church is gone." For the sake of peace, they just let the matter drop and Jane found accommodation elsewhere. Jane explains, "The rational part of me [said] that this would not be a good place to be living. I'd rather live in a tent."

Shortly afterwards, Marion began looking for another church, even though until then her ministry there had been a positive experience for her and the congregation. "I knew from that incident that I wasn't going to be there for a long time. I'd do the three years and then I'd be actively looking. I didn't want to live apart from Jane. We'd find a way to be together."

The congregation never knew that Marion and Jane were in a relationship except by hearsay. Proven fact, however, isn't always what counts. Sometimes gossip and assumptions, however unfounded, are all it takes to create problems. "Lisa" and "Carla" were good friends, just that, nothing more, when they decided to move in together. And that's the way it stayed. Carla needed a place to stay. Lisa, a United Church minister, didn't like living alone in a huge, empty manse. There were all sorts of good reasons to share the space.

The fact that the two women were just friends didn't stop the rumours and allegations in the community, however. Things started to get a little tense. Several people privately approached Lisa to let her know what was being said about her. Lisa felt torn. "I could have simply denied the rumours, but simply denying doesn't always stop the speculation," she explains, "and I didn't think it was really any of their business. Besides which, there are a lot of people who can't get off that easy, except by lying." It was partly out of a sense of solidarity with women who are couples that she eventually chose to say nothing. "I decided to wait. If people wanted to raise it with me directly, then fine, we'd talk about it. But as long as they were just talking about me behind my back, I wasn't going to raise it." Things have quieted down, and Lisa has gotten on with the work of ministry. Maybe people are still upset, who knows? As far as she can tell, everything is fine.

The fear of "what if" still keeps some United Church clergy so deep in the closet that no one knows, or even suspects. "Claire" is young and, as far as anyone in her congregation knows, single. "Sometimes I think, 'how could they not know?'" she says, "but I really don't think they do." Would-be matchmakers in the community are still trying to line her up with eligible young men.

In her part of the country, most gay and lesbian couples keep a very low profile, especially those in ministry. There is one woman in the congregation whose daughter is lesbian, but that's not generally known. Claire sometimes has people tell her "we don't have gay people in this community," and yet she knows of at least one parent. Claire lives with the constant fear of being found out and what that would mean. "I always find I'm playing a balancing act," she says. "I'm living in a fish-bowl." The church office is in the manse, and people often drop by to do photocopying. She has to be very careful of the messages on her answering machine, letters or cards she receives, even what's on her bookshelf. She finds herself asking what to do with personal letters. "I don't want to destroy everything that's sent to me, but it feels risky to keep them." How does she keep sane? "I find small spaces, where my partner and I are able to be who we are. I give myself 100 per cent to the work of ministry, but at the same time, it's not 100 per cent of who I am. There's always a piece held back." But Claire's learnt how to live with that; she's done it all her life.

At the extreme opposite end of the scale is the Rev. Erin Shoemaker. Shoemaker has been about as public about her sexual orientation as anyone could be. "I have never wished to be back in the closet," she says. "I couldn't be there if I tried. There are pros and cons, but I would never choose to not be who I am, in the church or out of it."

In 1996, the 52-year-old mother of three was featured in the *Globe and Mail*. She and her partner, the Rev. Sally Boyle, have been public about their relationship for many years. Boyle, also a United Church ordained minister, told Saskatchewan Conference that she was lesbian in 1988. She was president of Saskatchewan Conference in 1994, the year Shoemaker was ordained.

Because Shoemaker was over 50 when she was ordained, she was free to seek her own call. She was interviewed by St. Andrew's Pastoral Charge in Balcarres, a little congregation in the Qu'appelle Valley of Saskatchewan. Shoemaker assumed it would be one of a long series of interviews in her search for a congregation that would take her. Initially, she was amazed at how smoothly things proceeded. The pastoral relations committee liked her, she liked the congregation. In March 1994, the congregation voted and the call was issued.

Some people on the committee knew about Shoemaker's sexual orientation—it would have been common knowledge for any members at St. Andrew's who were involved with presbytery or Conference levels of the church—but some didn't know. The topic didn't come up in the interview. Shoemaker had decided that she would be honest with people if they wanted to talk with her about it, but that she would not raise it herself. The rules for dealing with a call don't require that sexual orientation must be disclosed. In fact, United Church policy says that "it is inappropriate to ask about the sexual orientation of those in the candidacy or call/appointment process." The complications in this situation arose because Shoemaker's relationship with another woman was well known in some circles. It was only a matter of time before word got back to St. Andrew's.

After the call went through, but before Shoemaker arrived, news of her sexual orientation got out. Some people in the congregation began demanding that her call be rescinded, because they hadn't been told she was a lesbian before they voted. Shoemaker says she didn't have anything to hide, and didn't try to hide, but some members of the congregation felt angry and betrayed. They wondered why those members of the committee who knew about Shoemaker and Boyle hadn't said anything. Others believed that a person's sexual orientation is simply not a relevant consideration in choosing a minister, so why would they have raised it?

Lana Brandow chaired the committee that called Shoemaker. She feels the committee was very thorough in following the correct procedures for issuing a call. Gordon Jardine, a member at St. Andrew's, says that the selection committee was unanimous in thinking that Shoemaker's abilities were exceptional. They hired her on the basis of competency, he says. "Even the ones who later said, 'over my dead body' would still say she's competent," he says.

Brandow has lived in Balcarres for 25 years. Even so, some people in the community still consider her to be "from away." She and her husband run the local veterinary clinic. The Brandows have a number of lesbian or gay people in their circle of friends. They feel it's important for their children to know and appreciate differences. Says Brandow, "I'm not afraid that our children will be corrupted, only that their lives will be made richer by having known a lot of different people."

Brandow feels that being part of the United Church, as she has most of her life, is exactly where she needs to be. She speaks in glowing terms of "this fabulous church of ours, struggling for justice, struggling to help us move to a higher level of regard and respect and inclusion. That fits my life, that fits like a good glove!" She went through some difficult times in the aftermath of the decision to call Shoemaker. There was a lot of anger. Some people stopped talking to her. Several key families left the church. That's a big issue in any congregation, but even more so in a small, closely knit congregation. When some people decided to leave, a lot of anger and grief spilled over into blaming Brandow and others on the committee for what happened. Brandow has a lot of empathy for the sense of loss. "Some people felt a deep sadness at this choice not to participate. Hey, who wouldn't feel sad when you know that so-and-so sat in that pew and they don't anymore? That's a loss—for us, for them."

Most people at St. Andrew's seem to think that if Shoemaker's orientation had been known in the whole congregation, she would never been called there. Some people in the congregation felt they had a right to that information. If all had been known, they say, the congregation might have felt more empowered in the process and there wouldn't be that lingering sense of hurt and betrayal. But Shoemaker wouldn't be there now. On the other side of the argument, because the information didn't come out until later, some people had a chance to meet and interact with a person of a different sexual orientation whom they would otherwise never have known. Shoemaker herself still questions which was the right path. "I have wondered over the years if the strategy I used in the call was the best one," she says. "But I've figured that there is no 'best one.' You come out and certain things happen. You don't come out and other things happen." It is clear that the United Church is still breaking new ground in this area, trying to figure out which paths are healthiest and fairest in the long run for congregations and clergy.

Marion Best thinks there is still need for structural work on the church's part. There need to be some supports in place, she thinks, to help gay and lesbian people as they struggle with coming out or not in particular situations. To whom can they talk? How would they know if a given context is supportive or not? How can decisions be made with integrity? What helps are in place if things do fall apart? Who is there to help congregations work through their very complex responses? A decade after the 1988 decision, the United Church is still working its way through a maze of complex issues.

Shoemaker found her first six months at St. Andrew's very hard. "I spent my first weeks doing pastoral care with people who didn't want me to be here," she says. At the first annual meeting after she started there was another move to have her ministry rescinded. Someone stood up at the meeting and made a motion, saying that it wasn't anything against Shoemaker personally, just that the congregation didn't want a homosexual minister. The motion was defeated, and the man found a church home elsewhere. Now, four years later, Shoemaker feels things are "pretty much like normal ministry." People in the congregation now fully acknowledge the presence of Boyle. "People ask about her when she's not here," says Shoemaker. "They treat us very much as a couple." Some people who were strongly opposed to Shoemaker and Boyle's presence in the community have become their friends.

Jardine thinks things at St. Andrew's have calmed down now. Even as little as a year ago, some board members might have thought it an advantage to get rid of Shoemaker. Now, they don't seem to think so. "It's not that huge word 'homosexual' anymore, it's just Erin, it's just our kids, it's just people."

Audrey Stephens, another congregational member, agrees. "We've settled down," says the 78 year old. "We are very much enjoying our minister and appreciating her gifts. I have always been of the opinion that people should be judged for who they are as a person, not by preconceived notions of a whole group. Those who are opposed quote those Old Testament passages that have been quoted to them, but they never read the whole chapter. For me, Christianity is not about judging others. It's about loving." Stephens was very happy with the decision to call Shoemaker. "I thought it would be a good experience for the whole congregation to know someone personally." Indeed, many people have changed their opinion after having come to know Shoemaker and Boyle. Now, there are more pressing things to deal with at St. Andrew's. Like most rural Saskatchewan churches, it has an aging and declining membership due to changing demographics and rural depopulation, and it has a big deficit.

Shoemaker survived in ministry at Balcarres, but the story is hardly a tale of "happily ever after." Situations like hers account for why so many United Church clergy who are lesbian or gay don't disclose that fact to their congregations. There are probably at least 200 clergy currently serving in congregations who have not come out in any public way. It's easy to see why. Who would want to go through that kind of turmoil, risk, and personal pain, knowing there is no sure outcome, and no guarantee of another job elsewhere if things fall apart. The problem is, as long as most clergy remain closeted, there is less impetus for the church to change and far greater risks and costs for those who do choose to come out.

Allison Rennie recognizes the dilemma, but is troubled by it nonetheless. "I really want this not to sound judgemental. I am aware of a number of extremely gifted people in the order of ministry and lay people in paid accountable ministry who are gay and lesbian. They are competent, doing excellent ministry. They are well received in the communities they serve and yet they are in the closet. They are living in fear of their relationships being discovered, of being outed."

While Rennie knows there are lots of valid reasons to be discreet about sexual orientation she finds herself feeling frustrated. "If we as gay and lesbian people don't hold the church accountable for its statements about inclusion I don't believe we can expect all the other people in the community to do it on our behalf," she says. "I want the church to be accountable for the things it says. Part of the way we are complicit in continuing homophobia is by staying in the closet. I know it's easy for me to say that because I was outed, I'm reconciled to that and I'm really happy. It's so much easier to live this way!" Rennie's impatience is understandable. Despite 1988, the United Church is not always as welcoming and inclusive as its official policy might imply. And most gay and lesbian members and clergy aren't ready to trust the church to find out what openness may exist. Twenty years ago, they were just barely beginning to trust one another.

13

BUILDING A MOVEMENT

Just as a rainbow isn't a rainbow without the full spectrum of the Divine Artist's palette, a church is not a church without the full spectrum of the Divine Artist's human creation.

barb janes

A woman from St. Thomas-Wesley United, a Saskatoon church that recently completed the Affirming Congregation Program, has taken to wearing an Affirm United button that says, "The United Church of Canada supports lesbian, gay and bisexual people." She wears it proudly on her coat. One day she went into a specialty cake shop. As the clerk was serving her, the young man said, "You know, it's so nice to see you wearing that button. I'm a gay man, and it sure is good to see your support." She still talks about the significance of that encounter, a conversation made possible because of a small action she decided to take.

In the 1970s, lesbian and gay United Church people began to form groups for mutual support. Many of them were serving as United Church clergy or in other leadership positions. They were anxious about the ferment around sexual orientation that was building in the church, and scared about the future. They came seeking support, and to remind themselves that they were not totally alone. The gatherings were publicized by word of mouth, and members took various precautions to secure the confidentiality of those present. Most of those who joined groups were not out; very few people were in those days. There were often surprise encounters at the meetings—friends and colleagues meeting up with one another at a gathering and discovering that someone they'd known for awhile was "one of them." Gary Paterson recalls the first meeting he attended. "I was astounded at who else showed up," he remembers, "and they all said 'WHAT!' when I arrived." Most people at that time knew nothing of his sexual orientation.

In 1982, the United Church General Council was held in Montreal and, for the first time, the issue of sexual orientation and ministry was on the agenda—the result of petitions from four Conferences. By then, there were small groups of gay and lesbian United Church people meeting in at least five cities. The Montreal group invited gays and lesbians from across the church to meet for a few days before the Council meeting to discuss the possibility of forming a national organization. Less than a dozen people gathered that first evening, in the upper room of the Newman Centre on Peel St., near the McGill University campus. A few more people arrived the next day, to reach a total of less than 25. In spite of the gathering's small size, emotions ran high: joy, excitement, relief and fear. Says one attendee, a theological student at the time, "I was quite terrified to be there!"

By the end of the three-day meeting, the group had decided to found Affirm: Gays and Lesbians in The United Church of Canada. The initial statement declared that:

"Affirm is a worshipping community celebrating the biblical and theological liberation which recognizes lesbians and gay men as members of the whole people of God. It is our purpose: to affirm gay men and lesbians within The United Church of Canada; to provide a network of support among regional groups; to act as a point of contact for individuals; and to speak to the church in a united fashion, encouraging it to act prophetically and pastorally both within and beyond the church structure."

Affirm had other organizational models on which to draw. "Dignity" had just formed as a Roman Catholic organization. The Anglican Church had "Integrity," and the Lutheran Church had an organization called "Lutherans Concerned." These other denominational organizations were formed by gays and lesbians and their supporters. Affirm was different, riskier, some say more daring, because it identified itself as a lesbian and gay group. All those who joined Affirm were lesbian, gay or bisexual. For some people, even having their name on the organization's confidential mailing list was an enormous step. To attend a meeting meant coming out, at least to the others present in the room.

The existence of Affirm as a group of gay and lesbian United Church people was very significant. After it was created came the difficult but even more significant decision to tell the church and the world that the organization existed. On the second day of the Montreal General Council meeting, Affirm issued a statement announcing its formation to the Council and to the media. There was an article on Affirm in the newsletter that was given to General Council commissioners. The story was immediately picked up in the national Canadian press. Almost immediately, the existence of Affirm made the presence of gays and lesbians in the United Church very real and very visible. For such a small group it had a surprisingly large impact. It gave voice and humanity to the issues the church was starting to discuss, and it refused to go away.

Affirm also provided a place of connection for gays and lesbians in the church who wanted to find each other. David Hallman was at the founding meeting and helped draft the press release. His room number at the General Council meeting was posted for anyone who wanted to contact the new organization. A few commissioners dropped by, "very discreetly," Hallman recalls. "They wanted to get in touch simply because they were homosexual, very closeted, and needed someone to talk to." For some, this was the first time they had told anyone.

Taking seriously its statement of purpose, Affirm attempted to speak to the United Church about the concerns of its constituency. Over the years, it submitted statements and briefs to different task groups working on human sexuality, sexual orientation, human rights, same-gender benefits, worship resources and resources for welcoming and inclusive congregations. Threaded throughout this work were stories of the oppression gay and lesbian people experienced in society and particularly in the United Church.

Affirm provided an important voice in the debate about human sexuality—a voice from within the church. "Affirm has always been trying to stay in the church, not threatening to leave," says Bill Siksay, one of the people who attended the founding meeting. "We have always been saying, we want to be here as full members. People saw that; they saw people struggling to stay in the church." Siksay was at the 1984 General Council in Morden, Manitoba, and witnessed what he considers to be a real turning point for the church. "Nineteen eighty-four showed decision makers in the church that it was possible to do something positive," he says. "They came to the 1984 General Council saying ordination of homosexuals is impossible. Commissioners after '84 in Morden left saying, 'I know it's the right thing to do; now I have to figure out how we accomplish it.' There was a real change in the people who were there over the period of that Council." When asked why he thinks this happened, Siksay replies, "Church people listening! To gay and lesbian people, to 'ex-gays,' to all the voices. Affirm held a meeting with the sessional committee dealing with that issue. At first it was only

Tim Stevenson and me, and then 15 people walked in and people saw old friends and long-standing colleagues. I don't think that committee could have done anything different."

❦

It's June 1988. The year of The Issue. Most of the delegates at the Conference meeting have taken the night off from the business of speeches, petitions and resolutions. Sixty or so have responded to the invitation to meet with Affirm to hear, first hand, the experience of gay and lesbian people. Two members of the regional group have agreed to speak. Neither of them is employed by the United Church, so they feel safe enough to do it. They talk about their lives, about discovering and struggling with their sexuality, about the experience of being an invisible minority. "People talk about 'those homosexuals' as though we're not here, not in our church," say one woman. It's her first time speaking to a group as a lesbian. She's decided it's worth the risk. The gathering adjourns. There's juice and coffee, but most people head off to their rooms. A few remain, clustering in small circles, to ask more questions and ponder where the United Church is heading.

Affirm always has had some national spokespeople willing and able to be out as gays and lesbians to speak to the larger church and the media. Many more members, while not able to be public to that degree, have participated in forums and discussions with Moderators and church committees. This meant that, on almost every occasion the United Church discussed the issue of homosexuality and ministry, gay and lesbian people were there to speak for themselves. This was an ongoing reminder to the church that homosexuals are not a "them" but part of the "us." At the 1988 General Council, members of Affirm and the Community of Concern, a group strongly opposed to the ordination of homosexuals in the United Church, had breakfast together. The two groups didn't end up agreeing. They did eat together, and talk. They recognized that they were part of the same church. That, in itself, was an accomplishment.

Affirm has sometimes been referred to as a large, well-funded lobby group. It isn't. Affirm started small, and has remained so, a rather loose affiliation of a dozen or so local groups across the country. It has never had staffing or office space, and has always existed from year to year on a shoe-string budget—enough to put out a quarterly newsletter, organize an annual meeting and conference, and hold one other meeting a year with representatives from local groups. It has struggled with communication, with getting organized within such an informal structure, with finding enough time and energy to get done what needed to be done, and always with too little money. The newsletter is still the primary communication link, with information about local activities, updates on what's happening in different parts of the church, calls for action and morale boosts for gay and lesbian rights advocates. For more isolated gay and lesbian United Church people, it is an important communication link and a reminder that there is a larger network of support out there somewhere.

The key to Affirm's success has been its visibility, its small but persistent presence where it counted—in congregations, presbyteries, Conferences and at General Council. Some people describe it as "leaven in the loaf."

Affirm has been visible, not so much through hard lobbying as with rainbow banners, colourful display tables and balloons. Affirm groups often engage in a kind of folk art of buttons, banners and bumper stickers. The organization has hosted wine and cheese parties, and joined in United Church Conference parades. At the 1988 General Council, Affirm set up a display table. Affirm members and supporters gave delegates not a position paper, but stories of real-life gay and lesbian people in the United Church. They also handed out pink lemonade—pink for the colour of the pink triangle. Like the yellow star for Jews, in war-time Germany the pink triangle was the sign that homosexuals were forced to wear in the Nazi death camps. It has become a symbol of resistance, and of gay liberation.

The idea of an organization called "Friends of Affirm" was conceived at Affirm's founding meeting. It became a larger network of people across the country who supported Affirm financially, emotionally and theologically. The Friends of Affirm movement has been vital in the changes that have taken place in the United Church. In some locations, Friends of Affirm created a local group to organize educational events and to act together with Affirm on projects and vigils. During a time when the debate in the United Church was at its most heated, one Friends of Affirm group started the "Let's Talk" campaign. They handed out buttons that said simply "Let's Talk" to anyone who would wear them. Many people did wear the buttons, as a sign that they hadn't closed their minds, as a sign that they were willing to be in dialogue with people with whom they might disagree, as a sign that they were lesbian or gay and willing to share their experience, as a sign that they were straight and willing to listen or be supportive, as a sign that the church would get through, because its members were still willing to talk to one another. Some people still wear that button, because the conversation isn't over yet.

It's 1989 and Affirm members have gathered for their seventh annual meeting. The group is at a low ebb this year, tired after all the intense work that led to the 1988 United Church decision, discouraged because the issues have not gone away. Gay and lesbian United Church folk are being blamed for the state of the church's finances, the decline in membership, the loss of some congregations, the ongoing conflict. Anti-homosexual attitudes in some places are even more intense. Opposition groups are calling for another vote at next year's General Council. It's likely the whole debate will be reopened! One lesbian woman tells the group how she recently applied to be a minister in a congregation. She was the first choice of the pastoral relations committee, and she was asked to sign a statement that she was not homosexual. She didn't sign. She's now unemployed, and needs some personal support just to get her through. And so the group gathers, a bit of a "ragtag bunch" as one person recalls, in a small room in a church basement to eat a meal together. The meal is special. It has become a tradition at Affirm annual meetings. They eat roast lamb with unleavened bread, and tell the story of the Exodus. The biblical themes of the Exodus and the wilderness resonate deeply, for they are powerful symbols of their own faith journeys. In the story they find images of hope, of a God who can lead them out of oppression into a new land. And they find images that others might miss, images of diversity. It is a "mixed" crowd (Exodus 12:38) that leaves Egypt under God's guiding hand. Not a uniform, one-dimensional group, but a gathering of people who are not all the same, who don't always agree, who don't always get it right, and yet who are God's beloved and holy people. It's a vision of church, a church where everyone doesn't have to be the same, where even gays and lesbians can be included, a church on its way to a promised land.

On its tenth Anniversary in 1992, Affirm and Friends of Affirm began discussing merging the two groups and creating a new organization. In 1994 a decision was made to formally create a new organization within the United Church called "Affirm United" to replace Affirm and Friends of Affirm. Nineteen ninety-two was also the year Affirm and Friends of Affirm launched their most significant project, the Affirming Congregations Program. The program has seen a number of congregations embark on a study process with a view to welcoming and including gay, lesbian and bisexual persons in all aspects of the congregation's life and work.

Delegates to the 1997 annual meeting of Affirm United put aside papers, budget sheets and laptop computers. At this meeting they have focused on the Affirming Congregation Program. Speakers from several churches have talked about their experiences. The group has discussed how to encourage more churches to get involved in the program, how to keep the church talking and how to provide better communication and support to the program. In spite of ongoing logistical hassles, there is great excitement about the number of churches that have signed up or shown interest, about the energy and hope the program has generated and about the difference the program is making, both in individual congregations but also in the wider church. But now it's time for worship. Someone lights a rainbow-coloured candle. The group sings a hymn and hears a scripture passage. Then someone drapes another coloured ribbon on a rainbow motif the group is creating. The rainbow reminds them of the storms through which they have travelled. Rainbows are also symbols of diversity: the many colours of the rainbow woven together into one, just as the church is woven out of many strands of diverse human experience. Affirm United continues to be a sign of diversity in the church, of diversity the United Church hasn't always welcomed but has decided not to exclude. The United Church has come a long way. In this gathering no one thinks it has "arrived," but the rainbow is also a sign of hope, an ongoing reminder of God's presence and promise, and of changes yet to come.

14

AFFIRMING CONGREGATIONS

You can't sing in harmony if everyone is singing the same note.

youth delegate, General Council 1997

Fourteen-year-old Mike has been asked to lead the children's conversation in church. The lectionary passage is 2 Samuel 1: 17-27, David's lament upon hearing news of the death of Saul and Jonathan. The passage includes verse 26: "I am distressed for you, my brother Jonathan; greatly beloved were you to me; your love to me was wonderful, passing the love of women." Mike is doing a "dry run" on Saturday afternoon, with his family members pretending to be the children listening in church. "So, do you think David and Jonathan were gay?" one of them asks provocatively. Mike pauses, but only briefly. "I was wondering about that myself," he says. "But anyway, I really don't think that's the point of the story." In church the following day, he tells the congregation what he thinks the story is really about. "It's about losing someone you love very, very much, and being totally sad when they're gone." For Mike, who has grown up in an Affirming Congregation, it's the love and loss that are important, not the gender or sexual orientation.

A couple of street people doze in the afternoon sun on the steps of an aging, red stone church, near the corner of Bloor St. and Spadina Ave. in downtown Toronto. Trinity-St. Paul's United Church is one of many inner-city churches that collaborate in an "Out of the Cold" program, which offers meals and shelter to homeless people. It isn't that cold today, so the street people are still outside. Inside the sanctuary, a huge rainbow banner proclaims "People of the Covenant." A bulletin board, also decorated with rainbows, announces "Welcoming Diversity." The building itself attests to that diversity. It houses a variety of cultural and social organizations, dance groups, the renowned Tafelmusik baroque orchestra and organizations addressing issues of poverty, violence against women and a range of other social change issues. The building is home to two United Church congregations: Trinity-St. Paul's, the larger of the two, and Bathurst St. United. Both congregations have another thing in common besides their shared building. They both recently became one of a dozen or so Affirming Congregations in the United Church.

Al Conery attends Trinity-St. Paul's. He has lived with his partner, Patrick, for four years. He was married for 22 years and has a daughter in her twenties. He continues to have a good relationship with his family but, like so many others, he had quite a struggle coming to terms with his sexual orientation. "I didn't want to be gay," he says forcefully, "but the more I fought against it the more stress it created. I wanted to fit in with everyone else. At age 46, I went to a group for gay fathers and found there were all kinds of gay fathers. Now I basically accept who I am. It's a better life for me because I'm not hiding anything any more."

Conery came from a Salvation Army background, but found he "couldn't be who he was" in that context. Still, he found himself longing for a church connection. He had heard about the United Church and its stance, and discovered that Trinity-St. Paul's had declared itself to be an Affirming Congregation. One Sunday morning, Conery showed up for worship there. As soon as he entered, he noticed a sign saying gays and lesbians were welcome in the congregation.

"I couldn't believe it," he says, the amazement evident in his voice. "It was so nice to see this going on. It made me feel good. You didn't have to skulk around and not let anyone know who you were. It drew me closer to the United Church because of what I saw there. "I wish I could have stayed with my own church," he says sadly. "I've been back, but they kind of beat up on you. I'd love to go to my local church and feel it's OK to be who I am. Patrick and I can go to Trinity-St. Paul's or Bathurst or Bloor St. or Glen Rhodes (other Affirming Congregations) and feel totally comfortable, and no one assumes we're brothers or friends or says 'bring your wife.'" Conery hopes the movement spreads. It would be good, he thinks, if other churches declared this kind of inclusive welcome.

Affirming Congregations in the United Church are local churches that welcome bisexuals, lesbians, gay men and their families in all aspects of church life. They are congregations that promote reconciliation for gay, lesbian and bisexual people, within the church and also in the larger society. And they are congregations that minister to and with people of all sexual orientations.

The Affirming Congregations Program, modelled on similar ones in other denominations, was created to give greater visibility to those United Churches that offer a ministry of inclusion and welcome to gays and lesbians, but also to encourage all congregations to find ways to be more open in their welcome. Whenever gays and lesbians come out, they take an enormous risk, often losing friends, family members, jobs or security. A congregation that declares explicitly that it is welcoming can create a safer place for gays and lesbians to share who they are. The congregation takes on more of the risk, because there's no doubt the decision sometimes creates conflict and controversy. But congregations often find they gain new members and a renewed sense of ministry as a result of the experience.

Congregations joining the program agree to undertake a process of study and discussion. They consider what it means for them to be inclusive and welcoming; they look at the barriers and ways in which they might become more inclusive, they consider what ministry and outreach they can offer to and with gay and lesbian people, and they prepare an official congregational statement that declares their intention to be welcoming of all. Then there's a celebration!

Trinity-St. Paul's has travelled far since its earliest discussions of homosexuality. In the early '80s, the presence of an openly lesbian candidate put the issue squarely in front of the congregation. The debate at first was rancorous, at times painful.

In 1994, Trinity-St. Paul's embarked on a process to become an Affirming Congregation. It formed a committee to guide the process. In meetings and congregational study sessions they looked at all aspects of congregational life. In a series of educational sessions, members of the congregation were invited to watch videos, talk about their own feelings and hear personal stories. The final stage of the process included a review of the congregation's mission statement to specifically include lesbian, gay and bisexual people. An Affirming Congregation statement and affirmative action policy completed the process. The board approved a policy statement amending the congregation's mission statement. The new statement reads: "We affirm that all who seek to live faithfully, regardless of ability, age, ethnicity, gender, race, or sexual orientation are full participants and we urge all to take responsibility in the life, membership and leadership in the church."

While the congregation basically supported sexual orientation issues when it began the process, it also recognized that further work was needed to carry forward the work involved in becoming a congregation that affirms people of all sexual orientations, particularly in areas such as pastoral care, outreach to other congregations, awareness building and developing same-gender covenanting services. A policy change passed easily at the official board. Trinity-St. Paul's added a line to its masthead declaring itself an Affirming Congregation.

Loraine MacKenzie Shepherd is a member at Trinity-St. Paul's. She says the process of becoming an inclusive and welcoming congregation didn't just happen automatically. There was opposition, as well as lively discussion. She thinks that, overall, "it's a success story." The congregation continues to grow in numbers, with a healthy dose of new younger families. She doesn't think anyone had real doubts that Trinity-St. Paul's would become an Affirming Congregation. In the process of discovering what being inclusive really means, however, the congregation discovered other forms of exclusion that it needed to address. "We decided to continue the discussion," she says, "in order to explore other issues of inclusion—physical ability, race, gender, economic issues. We have been working on the issue of race and racism and that has proved much more explosive than issues of sexual orientation. Some people said they thought this would be harder, and it was. It's hard for people to recognize the racism in themselves."

MacKenzie Shepherd thinks the congregation has done a lot of work on issues of racism but still has a long way to go. The congregation set itself the task of developing processes for eliminating racism and other forms of oppression and discrimination, to "move closer to a vision of right, just, healthy, mutual relationships, and a celebration of diversity." The ability to embrace differences is an important sign of health in a congregation. Those that can cope with diversity are better equipped to deal with the conflicts that emerge in day-to-day decision making, or with the differences in faith and life experience that exist within every congregation. They are often better able to be a welcoming church home where all members can be themselves and dare to differ or disagree.

Augustine United, in downtown Winnipeg, is no stranger to diversity. As an inner-city congregation, it encounters people from all walks of life. Bethan Theunissen, the staff associate at Augustine, is a lesbian lay woman from South Africa with a Methodist background and Baptist and Mennonite theological training. Sunday morning worship reflects diversity as well. The beautiful polished wood and stained glass reveal the church's distinguished Presbyterian origins. There is a visible presence of gay and lesbian people—people from the neighbourhood and people whose roots go deep into Augustine's 100 or so years of history.

In 1995, Augustine made history when it became the first Affirming Congregation in the United Church. Although the congregation had studied and reflected on issues of sexual orientation for more than 20 years, it undertook four years of intense study and debate before its public statement and celebration as an Affirming Congregation. The first motion was rejected in 1993, not because people disagreed with the vision of inclusion, but because many people felt the congregation needed to do more work to become a truly safe and welcoming place for lesbians and gays. A statement in its Sunday worship bulletin reads, "Augustine is a community that welcomes, recognizes and accepts lesbian, gay and bisexual people in our midst as full and equal participants in all aspects of our life, work and worship."

St. Thomas-Wesley United, situated in an inner-city red light district of Saskatoon, became an Affirming Congregation in 1997. Elaine Findlay has been an active member for many years. She recalls the many heated and conflict-ridden debates in the congregation during The Issue years. There was one meeting in 1984 in which someone stood up and said, "I'm leaving" and someone else retorted, "Well, just do that then!"

Findlay thinks it's important to keep talking. She encouraged the congregation to consider becoming an Affirming Congregation because she believed that "the process of study is important whatever the congregation finally decides," she says. She hoped that the discussion might inject some new energy into a congregation in decline and in serious financial trouble. Some people asked, "Why are we working on this when there are so many other things that need attention?" Others worried that there wasn't much point in becoming affirming if the congregation was going to die anyway. "But now we see that this could be a way to bring new life to the congregation," she says. The discussions have been lively, though not so acrimonious as in 1984. Even with the congregation named an Affirming Congregation, Findlay doesn't think the process is over. "We're not there yet. This is just a beginning."

Affirming Congregations can have an important impact on their own members. Marie Marsellus has been United Church from birth. She grew up in Toronto, where she was very active in the Young People's Union. From that springboard, she continued to be involved in congregational life and leadership. She was in her sixties when she began a relationship with a woman and told her family and friends that she was lesbian. She knew about her sexual orientation "for a matter of fact" when she was 12 years old but, then, "what can you know in 1946?" she asks herself regretfully. What she knew in her gut was the feelings she had for women and girls.

Marsellus was active on different committees that were working on the issue of sexual orientation in the 1980s, but always assumed she would never come out. She doesn't know if she would have been prepared to take the risks, but for the supportive church community she found at Bloor St. United. For her, "it meant that if I stepped out, I'd be OK, I'd have a mattress to fall on and a hammock to rest on." She found the majority of that congregation to be very supportive. It also helped to have other models in the community of people who were open about their sexual orientation. She recalls with gratitude the people "who can stick it out and do their thing and be who they are. It affects the slow ones like myself."

She is grateful to finally be out with her family, and to feel their support. Her own children were by then in their thirties, and her parents in their early eighties. Some of her friends were initially shocked and surprised. "There are probably others in your life that you don't know either," she told them.

Marsellus was a strong advocate for Bloor St. United beginning the Affirming Congregation process. "Some people felt we don't need to do this because we're already supportive," she says. But she felt it was very important to be a positive and public model for other churches. "Other folk may not be willing or able to act on it right away. But the more we are out, the more models there are for those who come after. It may take two or three years for people to evolve, but that's why the church setting is so important, because then it spins out into the world."

The Rev. Warren McDougall, one of the ministers at Bloor St., agrees. "It's really important to make a public statement," he says. "Because of all the damage that has been done in the past, we need to say something really strong."

Kay Heuer was on the Affirming Congregation committee at Bloor St. She says the committee's task was to reopen the congregation to something they thought they had already accomplished. "We had to convince some people of the validity of making this an official statement," she explains. The final wording of the statement was hammered out over several meetings. It now says, "We believe that all people are created in the image of God and are unconditionally loved by God. All persons are free to enjoy God's gifts of love, joy and intimacy."

Heuer sees the statement Bloor St. made as a witness, a way of taking responsibility for action. "It means not only [that this is] what we believe," she says. "It means we're willing to hire gays and lesbians, to be part of the network, to make our liturgy inclusive." The Bloor St. statement commits the congregation to "creating a community where all people are welcome regardless of age, gender, race, sexual orientation, differing abilities, ethnic background, or economic circumstance ... We pray for God's Spirit to guide us as we work for reconciliation and justice for all persons in both church and society."

For most of the Bloor St. congregation, sexual orientation is not a matter of tremendous public debate. Gay and lesbian people are involved and integrated at all levels of congregational life. There isn't really a sense of a separate group. "We don't really talk that much about it any more," says McDougall. After all, the congregation has been working on the issue for more than 20 years now. "It's only shocking for people who are visiting who don't know what they are getting themselves into," he says, recalling the look on the faces of some visitors the Sunday that a baby was baptized—a baby who'd just been adopted by two men.

Bloor St. United was a significant place for Gwen Chapman and Mary-Ellen (M.E.) Kish. They were both guitar-playing types in the young adults group, and got to know each other while planning music for a worship service. They were both in the very early stages of coming out when they came to Bloor St. in the late 1980s. "Bloor St. helped us come out to ourselves and to each other," says Kish. "This was a church community where it was OK for us to talk about what we were feeling and experiencing. There was a supportive community there saying, 'It's OK for you to be who you are.'"

When Kish and Chapman moved to Vancouver after completing graduate studies, they went as a couple. Leaving Bloor St. was hard. They had a sense that they weren't going to find another congregation exactly like it in Vancouver. They looked for a church where they could be comfortable as a lesbian couple, and found one at St. James United Church, which later amalgamated with Kitsilano United to form Trinity United. Kish and Chapman co-chaired the board of the newly formed congregation. And somewhere along the line they got the idea that, before their term was up, they would initiate an Affirming Congregation process at Trinity. The congregation already had a history of supportive involvement on the issue. One of the ministers, Linda Ervin, was openly lesbian. The congregation had been celebrating covenanting services for same-gender couples for several years.

While not everyone may have felt totally comfortable, issues of sexual orientation weren't much of an issue. "It's fine for them to come here," one older member was heard to say. Then, with some exasperation, she added, "I just wish they'd sign up for ushering!" The congregation held a series of story-telling Sessions and Bible studies on the theme, and worked on a statement of inclusion.

In April 1997, Trinity United held a service of celebration. "We had this wonderful service, and people maybe got more of a sense then of how important this was to gay and lesbian people and the community, partly because the church was so full and there was such high energy," Kish says. "People from gay and lesbian and bisexual communities showed up, those for whom it was really important that a church was doing that." Jews and Anglicans attended, as well as people from other denominations. The Vancouver gay and lesbian choir sang, and Bill Siksay spoke on behalf of M.P. Svend Robinson. Many people in the congregation realized they'd done something bigger than they'd thought. The congregation gained a few new members. One young man said, "I have been looking for a church for a long time. When I heard about the stance you had taken, I knew this was a place I wanted to be a part of."

One phrase of the Trinity's new mission statement is especially important to Chapman and Kish. It's the part that says Trinity will "honour each other's life passages in liturgy and celebration , including covenanting ceremonies, dedication of children, rituals of baptism, healing, death and dying." That's because they are facing a new passage in their own lives. "The next step in our coming out process is that we're going to have a baby," Chapman says, her face glowing with excitement. "I'm pregnant!" They both know that, when the time comes for them to have their child baptized, there will be no question that they will be recognized, and celebrated, as its parents.

For Trinity United in Vancouver, to be an Affirming Congregation meant not only affirming lesbians and gays but all those who are exiled, homeless or voiceless. In December 1995, the church agreed to a request for sanctuary from a Salvadoran woman, Maria Baharona, and her five children, all under the age of 11.

Baharona had been an activist during El Salvador's civil war. When her life was threatened by death squads, she escaped to the United States. In 1991, as the American Immigration and Naturalization Service began a round-up of illegal immigrants, she came to Canada where she claimed refugee status. Her claim was denied. She and her family were given sanctuary in the Trinity United Church basement for almost two years. When she was finally deported in August 1997, the congregation worked with Salavadoran churches to help secure her safety, and committed itself to raising more than $30,000 to aid her resettlement. Clearly, being an Affirming Congregation meant more to Trinity than including and supporting just one group.

Several times in its long history, Glen Rhodes United Church, a congregation in the east end of Toronto, went through an amalgamation. Twice it sold an extra building to the Metropolitan Community Church, a gay and lesbian church. The first time that happened was in 1984, and initially there was a bit of a stir. Metropolitan Community Church was the highest bidder, but some people still objected. Until one elderly choir member stood up and said, "I know that it's hard for people to accept. I had a friend and I'm sure she was, well, you know..." She couldn't quite say the words. "But I remember who she was and how I treated her, and I'm ashamed, and I don't want to say no now." The church property was sold to Metropolitan, and it was the first time in the history of the denomination that they had been permitted to purchase a church building. The second time the issue came up, there wasn't even a ripple.

When the Affirming Congregation Program came to Glen Rhodes, people were ready. The Rev. Lawrence Pushee has been at Glen Rhodes since 1980. He has seen the congregation through several of its amalgamations. He sees each amalgamation as a kind of shake-down, a cleansing process that helped people prepare to embrace the future. In his view, this helped pave the way for the Affirming Congregation process.

In the early '90s, Glen Rhodes went through another re-evaluation that included Bible study and reflecting on its mission, as it began once again to discuss amalgamating. That's when they started looking at who their neighbours were, and what it meant to break down barriers—physical and social—and to be fully inclusive. They called it "the Greening of Glen Rhodes." In February 1996, they held a special service to celebrate the years of study that led to them becoming an Affirming Congregation.

The Rev. Susan Thompson is one of the ministers at Glen Rhodes. For her, looking back on the 1980s as an ordained lesbian feels like remembering a nightmare. Terrified that the discovery of her lifestyle would lead to the end of ministry within the church, she lived in isolation, fear and growing depression. There was a devastating moment when, after eight years in a congregation, the grandfather of a child she had just baptized looked into her eyes and told her he would leave the congregation if a homosexual minister were ever called. She felt invisible. Unable to be open about her true self, it was hard to be fully authentic. She felt that her ministry suffered.

The price she paid for not being out was often high. She went through the breakup of a seven-year relationship without anyone in the congregation knowing. But, as the church began to change in the '90s, so did her life. "Imagine my joy," she says, "when called to a church already preparing to begin the Affirming Congregation process! Being loved and accepted in this congregation has restored my faith, enlivened my ministry and helped me to 'become the girl God would have me be!'" she says, quoting the motto of the United Church youth program Canadian Girls in Training.

The process already has borne fruit in other ways for Glen Rhodes. Several new families have joined because the parents want their children to grow up in an unprejudiced environment. One person returned after 50 years of being out of the church. "I'm coming back because now it's my church," he said.

Two gay men live down the street from Glen Rhodes, in an area with a somewhat "redneck" reputation. They both had a church background, but had long since given up on the church. That is, until they saw the inclusive welcome on the Glen Rhodes sign. The men had been receiving death threats from some local teenagers. They wanted to have a community dinner and to invite everyone on the street, as they put it, "to get to know who your queers are in your neighbourhood." They asked Glen Rhodes for help and, to their amazement, the church responded positively. Sixty people from Rhodes Avenue came to dinner—a pot luck supper at Glen Rhodes United— each wearing his or her street number on a name tag. They sat in the church hall beneath a banner that said "Glen Rhodes, journeying towards becoming an Affirming Congregation," and talked about how they could make their community safer and more welcoming for everyone. The "Greening of Glen Rhodes" became the flowering of a new sense of community that went well beyond the bounds of its church building.

15

CHANGE OF HEART

Never doubt that a small group of thoughtful, committed citizens can change the world—indeed, it is the only thing that ever has.

Margaret Mead

Sometimes the longest part of a journey is from the head to the heart.

Stan McKay

"I have an 89-year-old mother who lives in a community a few miles from Morden, Manitoba. Her church used to be a member of the Alliance of Covenanting Congregations [a fellowship of about 100 United Churches that are opposed to gays and lesbians in ministry]. In 1984, General Council was at Morden and I was involved as one of the organizers. One group of commissioners was coming to Winnipeg to be guests of the gay church. They would be taking in a Gay Pride Day parade as part of that experience. I went out to see my mom. 'If anything is in the papers, this is the only thing anyone will be interested in. I just wanted you to know this is the stuff that will be talked about, this is what I'll be saying to the press.'

"She kind of looked at me and said, 'So where did you think I'd be on that issue?'

"'I don't know,' I said. 'It hasn't exactly been dinner-time conversation.'

"'It's about time the United Church put its money where its mouth is. We had a gay minister once and we were just terrible to him.'

"'I knew—I didn't know you did,' I said.

"My mom suffered a lot in 1988. Petition after petition was going to General Council. Her friends would come and ask her to sign and she wouldn't. At one time, she was the only person who didn't sign a petition. She lost a lot of friends over that. She still lives there and it's been tough. I think there are people all over who stood up for what they believe in very quiet ways, and I think she's one of them. She would never make a speech, she would never tell them they're out to lunch. People like her won't be heard in the big debates, but they are there in all communities. As long as they and lots more like them can quietly make their stand, then maybe there will be real transformation."

❦

In 1984, a United Church family with four teenagers debated the issue of homosexuality vigorously around the dining room table. Dad, an ordained minister, argued that homosexuality was a form of mental illness, not "natural." Two older teens, having met lesbians and gays at university, disagreed. Mom wasn't sure. The youngest, 13, got out his Bible for the first time in a while to look at what it actually said. Twelve years later, they are still talking. This time, though, it's about the upcoming same-gender covenanting celebration of the middle daughter. Mom is busy making dresses. The service is being planned. Some of the uncles and aunts will be there, along with a sprinkling of cousins. They are looking forward with excitement to this family celebration of love and commitment. The family has been through a lot of changes in its attitude to sexual orientation.

Why some people changed their minds and some didn't remains one of the mysteries of the United Church's struggle with The Issue. One factor, although by no means the only one, is a person's experience with people who are gay and lesbian. Most major shifts in attitude seem to come out of a personal encounter with someone who is homosexual. Often, in the case of families, it is an unavoidable and painful discovery. It can take a while to travel through the kind of upheaval created when a close family member comes out of the closet.

Bill and Inez Walker know what that's like. Bill says he had a hard time initially accepting the fact that his son, Russell, was gay. "I've come around, but it's taken me a while," he acknowledges. His wife agrees, "We certainly had to change our thinking." The hardest part, she says, is when other people aren't accepting. It has been especially hard in their church community, a fairly conservative place. As Bill points out, "There's still a lot of opposition to homosexuality in Alberta."

Russell Walker grew up in the same congregation his parents still attend. As one of the few teens in the congregation, he got a lot of support and affirmation. It was a good place to grow up. In 1983, the congregation supported him as a candidate for ministry. That was before Russell knew he was gay and moved to Toronto, before he met his partner, Brian.

Bill and Inez talk quite openly about their son's relationship, and about their new grandson, Russell and Brian's adopted son, Tyler. Several people in the congregation ask about them, and see them as family, but they find some people still aren't very supportive, and many just don't want to talk about it. The congregation always has taken a position that homosexuality is wrong. On the other hand, they did send Russell and Brian a gift on their fifth anniversary. Bill thinks people may be coming around, "but it's a slow process," he admits. "They are aware of our situation, but they still have their own feelings. It's a real tough row to hoe."

Barbara Rumscheidt thinks the experience of personal connection with the pain is the basis for a lot of real conversion. She's a member of a PFLAG group. PFLAG stands for Parents and Friends of Lesbians and Gays, but in Rumscheidt's experience it's mostly mothers who come. They come, she says, "to talk about their own experience of finding out that a family member is gay or lesbian." They share their own shock or sorrow, their concerns about how the rest of the world will react, and their fears. "And suddenly," she speaks from experience, "you see. You see things differently." That's conversion, she believes. "It's a continual story. There's so much of that happening at the level of familial relationships."

Sometimes the conversion can be quiet dramatic. Charlotte Caron, on the faculty at St. Andrew's College, Saskatoon, recalls a student at the college, Norma Baumet, who was ordained in 1988. Baumet died a few years ago. She came into the college as a Free Methodist, but later joined the United Church. While at St. Andrew's, she came to a totally new view of faith, life and homosexuality. She became a strong supporter of lesbians and gay. Baumet believed in repentance, and when she came to the believe that she had been wrong in her views about gay and lesbian people—and that to be gay and lesbian is not sinful—her repentance was to work as strongly as she could in Friends of Affirm and to get involved in areas such as AIDS work. What she did was very risky at that time, but she was a married woman in her fifties. She felt that she was in a position where she had the obligation to speak because she was safe. Her conversion was a profoundly spiritual one. She began to open her eyes to see the world in a different way.

There is a large element of the unknown in conversion experiences in terms of why they happen sometimes and not others. Most people don't change their attitudes very quickly, or very much, even over a lifetime. And yet, there are many stories of profound change. Sometimes that change seems to have something to do with the movement of the Spirit.

The Rt. Rev. Bill Phipps was elected Moderator of the United Church in 1997, but he has been to many other General Councils and church gatherings, enough to have heard many stories of people who completely changed their minds and hearts around the issue of homosexuality. He recalls one sessional committee dealing with this topic at a General Council after 1988. On the same committee, there were gay and lesbian people and people who were fundamentally opposed to gay and lesbian people being in ministry or even in the church. The gay and lesbian people weren't out to the whole committee. Phipps watched a process of slow transformation. "After meeting for a few days, they trusted the group enough for their story to come out," he recalls. "I can remember some very sensitive, eyeball-to-eyeball, trying-to-understand-each-other conversations in the middle of a sessional committee of 25 people." In particular, he recalls one very conservative, middle-aged male minister and a young lesbian minister. "She was trying to get him to understand her life and he was really trying to understand, because he liked her. All of us watched this process for eight days."

Finally, the older man, a highly respected member of Maritime Conference, stood on the floor of General Council and talked about his conversion, and how he was going to have to go back to his congregation and talk to them. Phipps believes there was something larger happening in the sessional committee. "We all came out of there saying, 'We've seen the Spirit working between two people who really wanted to hear each other, who weren't there to pound each other over the head.' She wasn't telling him he was a bastard and he was wrong. She wanted him to understand her life. And he wanted to understand her life." Phipps believes that's conversion. Most changes in attitudes about homosexuality happen through experience, meeting people and getting to know them. But often it isn't quite that dramatic.

Lynette Miller has been an ordained minister in the United Church since 1973. Through her work in interim ministry, she has spent time with a lot of congregations and has seen a gradual shifting of attitudes. "As the process unfolds—of people discovering that someone they know and respect is gay—there is just a general softening." People may not move from strongly held opinions against homosexuality to immediately accepting the idea of gay and lesbian ministers, but they may take smaller steps along the way.

Barbara Rumscheidt knows of a congregation in the Maritimes that recently voted to have an openly gay man serve as an elder. The name was presented to the annual meeting. No one stood up and said they didn't think he should be an elder because he was gay. There was lots of talk behind the scenes. One man, in particular, had been very vociferous in his views about gay men, and quite vocal in the debate about homosexuality and ministry, she recalls. In the case of electing an elder, however, it was someone he knew. "'I didn't think we should have a minister who was gay,' he said, 'but that didn't mean I was saying no Sunday school teacher or elder or anyone else.' So he was making his own distinctions. You could see some changes."

In his 1995 book *The Bibby Report: Social Trends Canadian Style*, sociologist Reginald Bibby noted that, since the 1950s, Canadians have been "conscious of the need to be more open about sexuality." Attitudes definitely have changed, on sexuality in general and homosexuality in particular. Bibby measures what he calls the "approval rating" on homosexuality—the number of Canadians who believe that homosexual relations are not wrong at all or only sometimes wrong. In 1975, only 28 per cent of Canadians approved of homosexual relationships. In 1995, that figure had risen to 48 per cent. Bibby expects the number to reach 50 per cent shortly after the turn of the century and 60 per cent "in the foreseeable future." Canadian opinion about homosexuality is changing slowly, and more slowly in some places than others. Bibby found that in the Atlantic and Prairie provinces, Canadians expressed the greatest disapproval of homosexuality.

This change in the overall approval rating, however, is due only partially to individuals significantly changing their attitudes. Bibby notes that personal attitude change is much slower than these numbers would suggest—most people don't change their minds very much about major issues. What has happened, instead, is that there was a liberalizing of attitudes among the Baby Boomers in the 1970s. "They appear to have passed their views on to their children while becoming somewhat more accepting of homosexuality themselves during the past 20 years," explains Bibby. The Boomers' parents, on the other hand, who make up the bulk of the membership of the United Church, collectively have changed very little in their approval of homosexuality. The change in the approval rating reflects the demographics of the Canadian population as one generation ages and dies.

This would explain why some people believe that the United Church didn't change all that much when it made its historic 1988 decision. The church always has been rooted in a social justice ethos. It always has been very diverse in its membership, forged as it was from a union of different denominations. It always has been hesitant to exclude people at either end of the spectrum. It always has been fairly liberal and open to different points of view. It also has been fairly typical, reflecting the general attitudes of Canadian society. Perhaps Bill Siksay is right when he says that "the church didn't change when it did what it did. It was just being true to itself. It was being very typically United Church. It was more that it was true to its history and ethos than that it changed." That isn't to say that nothing changed.

Some people changed their minds dramatically. More often, people changed slowly and gradually, by talking about it and slowly, over a decade or more, coming to accept—or at the very least, being willing to live with—a decision that they didn't really like.

From his perspective as a staff person with British Columbia Conference, Brian Thorpe believes that, in the long run, the congregations that came out of The Issue years in the best shape were the ones that studied and openly discussed the issues. "I am firmly convinced that the congregations that did talk about it came out healthier than the ones that refused to raise the topic." These congregations seem to have fared better by facing their differences and disagreements openly, rather than keeping the issue under wraps for fear of conflict. They are much better off than those where people were told what to think, on either side of the issue—those congregations lost members in large numbers, or are still hurting to this day. For example, the congregation Brian Thorpe was serving in the late '80s and early '90s was among the 20 per cent in the United Church that did study the issues. In the fall of 1988, people met together in a further series of study Sessions to talk about what had happened. The congregation put a strong emphasis on talking about it. The result was that there was virtually no loss of members. No core families left and as the congregation turned the sod on a new building in the fall of 1988, many new families started attending.

Open-ended conversation was key to helping people come to terms with those difficult and sometimes painful changes in their church and their lives. When people were given room and time to form and express their own opinions, when they were not boxed in or forced to choose sides, congregations remained relatively intact. Some individuals slowly changed their minds. Those that didn't still found that they had a welcoming church home, one where all opinions, including theirs, could be respected.

Marion Best tried to model that kind of non-judgemental listening in her role with Sessional Committee Eight, back at the 1988 General Council. She continued to do so during her term as United Church Moderator. Best believes that people who are still upset with the United Church's decision have valid reasons for hurting. "I try to approach them with understanding," she says. "There must be a reason why you're where you are. I'd like to hear your story." In 1995, during the first year she was Moderator, she was invited to spend some time with a congregation that was quite upset with the United Church. She used this approach. They were really distressed about three things: that she was Moderator (since she had chaired Sessional Committee Eight and was associated with the 1988 decision); changing worship patterns; and inclusive language. "In 1988, their congregation split right down the middle, and they were still grieving the loss of those neighbours. They are a small community. They continue seeing those people at the corner store, at the post office. But they don't go to the same church any more. That still hurts."

When working on issues of sexuality, Best gave everyone a copy of the original 1988 decision and asked them to read it and note things with which they agreed and disagreed. A number of people were surprised. "We've never seen this before," they said. "We didn't know this is really what it said." It was seven years before they finally were able to look at the document and have a conversation about it. Best thinks these kinds of opportunities are really helpful in clearing the air. "Some of them were able to talk about what they had been taught about sexuality and how this felt like such a turnaround to them, and they did feel betrayed. And others were able to say, 'We have to talk about these people as human beings. How do we know God hasn't called these people?' These people were willing to go into the fear—seven years later."

Best believes that the process one uses to make decisions is vital to a healthy outcome in the long run. And good process takes time, time to build understanding, time to sit with things for a while, time to listen and time to talk. Sessional Committee Eight took lots of time. It met for three full days before Council began, then intensively throughout the Council meeting. It probably logged the most hours of any sessional committee. The core of its work was accepted, but the committee members had many more hours to struggle with the issues than the rest of General Council. They had a chance to really listen to each other and, under Best's leadership, to learn to respect each other even when they disagreed. The rest of the General Council commissioners had to debate at microphones and take a vote which, to her, "felt like creating winners and losers."

Best regrets that things couldn't have been done differently. "I remember one person who said that we had the advantage of being a part of the sessional committee," she says. "As part of the rest of the Council, they didn't have that opportunity. This should be a community learning how to honour and respect each other. I wish we could have worked more with the whole Council." In some ways, the rest of the church still may be taking the time it didn't have, in 1988, to catch up with the recommendations of Sessional Committee Eight.

Dorothy (Mundle) Naylor has been a diaconal minister since 1959. She grew up in Boston, but has spent most of her working life in Alberta. She's now working in a small congregation in southern Alberta, an area that was in what she describes as a "big uproar" in 1988. Naylor thinks it's partly that people didn't have enough time to consider the issue. They hadn't done any of the studies, they hadn't really talked about the issue of homosexuality at all and, all of a sudden, here was the church making a momentous decision. "They didn't like being surprised and they didn't like being put on the spot," she explains. "They didn't know why the church was even doing this. Because they hadn't done much reading or studying and because their own internal theological and biblical structure said 'no,' they really weren't equipped to take that kind of stand." They didn't even know anyone who was lesbian or gay, except those they read about in the newspapers. Now, a decade or so later, she says they have had more chances to think about it, more chances to meet people. Their young people are speaking up, young people who are not willing to see gays and lesbians in the same light. And there's someone in their congregation that they know. He's ordained, looking for a call, and he occasionally preaches for them. "It's OK, because people know him," Naylor thinks. "I have a sense people are now willing to accept and hear what he has to offer, even knowing he's gay."

Inez Walker doesn't put a lot of energy into trying to change people's opinions in her home congregation. Although it's still painful to have her son and his family devalued, she doesn't believe in hitting people over the head. She is, however, very active on an Alberta Conference committee working to keep the conversation going in the wider church. The committee, the Sexual Orientation, Pastoral Care and Justice Task Group, holds workshops, makes presentations at Conference, and helps share information about what is happening across the wider church. Members are there for support when individuals or congregations need it. They try to keep the issues on the church's front burner.

Nellie Spicer, another member of the Alberta Conference task group, has been around the church "quite a few years." (She doesn't say exactly how many.) She has been on the committee for five years, as well as serving in many other leadership roles in the church. Currently she's studying to be a diaconal minister. Her place of work and learning is the Claresholm-Stavely Pastoral Charge in the Foothills Presbytery. She didn't make any bones about letting the congregation know where she stood on The Issue. "When I was hired at Stavely, I said to the committee, I have the pink triangle on my wallet, and you know I work with this committee and this is my stance." She doesn't mince words. They hired her anyway—wallet, pink triangle and all.

Spicer was instrumental in getting a petition through Foothills Presbytery that eventually made its way to the 1997 General Council for action. Like all petitions, it has a rationale and a faith base. It cites Article 2:14 in the Basis of Union, which requires us to live lives of justice and compassion. It also lists various scripture passages that tell of Jesus welcoming and protecting children, and that point to Jesus' message of love that shows itself in action. "As Christians we believe that children and youth should be educated in a safe environment," it says. "All children and youth need their own sense of dignity and deserve to be treated with respect, love, understanding, sensitivity and acceptance for who they are." Then it goes on to urge school boards, governments and teacher's unions to develop policies and procedures to promote sensitivity, tolerance and safety for gay and lesbian students.

The petition was sparked by the real life situation of a woman on another committee who had a gay stepson. She watched how hard a time he had in school, and how much that affected him. Maybe if schools were safer and more accepting he wouldn't have had such a hard time, wouldn't have left for the city where he later contracted AIDS, Spicer speculated. Maybe a better school environment would have kept him closer to home and safer. Maybe, maybe not, but as a teacher, Spicer says she has seen a number of kids badly abused, called names like "faggot." "Whether they were or weren't, those kinds of words could be used freely and people in authority would just shrug and do nothing," she says. For Spicer, this is a justice issue. Change isn't just about changes in attitude—it's about structures and systems and advocacy in the wider world.

When the petition got to presbytery, there was a bit of discussion. Someone asked if they hadn't done enough on the issue already. Spicer thinks there were probably a few people who "shrugged their shoulders and said, 'here we go again!'" Someone wondered if this was interfering in the school system. Another person made a passionate appeal. "Until any kid can attend school freely and not be subjected to any kind of pressure, we need to do this," she said. "And when we're done we need to go to every school board so that every school kid in every school in Alberta is safe." The petition passed, with two opposing votes. General Council discussed it briefly and also agreed to act on its recommendations. That done, the task group has moved on to other things. Its members are currently planning a big national conference. They are quite excited—Svend Robinson has agreed to be a speaker.

Many of the 12 other United Church Conferences have committees similar to the one in Alberta Conference. They are usually small groups of people concerned about creating ongoing change in the church and in society. In 1993, Toronto Conference passed a resolution saying that by 1998, it would find 10 congregations that would be willing to have a gay or lesbian minister. A small committee was set up to find, or help create, those congregations. The work of the Toronto Conference Committee on Inclusive Ministry is to make contact with congregations, hold workshops, offer information and resources, provide support and information. They put up display tables at church meetings and leave pamphlets on the tables. One of their workshops was called "Sex Again." So far they've found six congregations, but they're not so much worried about the numbers as they are about an ongoing educational process. That's what one member of the committee, the Rev. Frank Hamper, thinks. "There has been a bit of a shift from the numbers game to getting the story out," he explains. "Our primary focus is on sexual orientation and ministry, helping people become more accepting, encouraging dialogue about the 'isms' and phobias that act as barriers to inclusive ministry."

Hamper knows the importance of dialogue. He is a minister at Fairbank United Church in North York, one of the six congregations identified as being inclusive. He was settled there in 1996 as an openly gay candidate from British Columbia Conference. His home Conference also passed a similar resolution "to find a minimum of 10 pastoral charges that will make themselves available for internship, settlement, appointment or call of any suitably qualified person regardless of sexual orientation." British Columbia Conference set up a committee that surveyed and interviewed a number of congregations in the Conference. In its final report, the committee said "there is a much higher level of openness to the prospect of gay and lesbian persons in ministry than we would have supposed." Of the first nine congregations the committee contacted, three already had openly gay and lesbian ministers in place and were satisfied with the experience, and five of the remaining six congregations felt their congregation would be willing to accept the recommendation of the pastoral relations committee if it recommended a lesbian or gay candidate.

The British Columbia Conference committee concluded its final report by noting the many similarities between the experience of gays and lesbians in ministry and the experience for women when they first entered ordained ministry 60 years ago. When women were first ordained, very few pastoral charges would have wanted one as their minister. "There are still many congregations where women are not accepted as equally competent to minister," says the report, "and women still experience particular stresses and difficulties, which cause some to grow discouraged and leave." Nevertheless, there is a growing acceptance of women in ministry, as the role of women in church and society continues to change. The committee hopes the same thing will happen for gays and lesbians. The report concludes, "We dare to hope that eventually, as is beginning to happen with women, the church will come to appreciate the particular gifts gays and lesbians bring for the enrichment of the whole body."

It's important to do advocacy within the church. It's equally important to address issues in the larger society. Rainbow Ministry does both. A project of Winnipeg Presbytery, it has a mandate to provide an outreach to the gay and lesbian community in the Winnipeg area. Ken DeLisle gives a few hours each week to the work of Rainbow Ministry. His partner, John Robertson, also works for the ministry 15 hours a week. As DeLisle explains, this isn't about converting people to religion. "There is a spiritual need in the gay and lesbian community," he says. "We try to identify needs and find ways the United Church might be able to assist." At the same time, the committee has a mandate to do education within the United Church, to be what he calls "a prophetic voice" in the church. The committee does everything from providing support and counselling to holding a workshop on spirituality on Gay Pride Day.

According to Joan McConnell, personnel minister for Manitoba and Northwestern Ontario Conference, "Rainbow Ministry has been one of the things that Winnipeg Presbytery did of which they should be proud. It didn't have a really hard time getting approved, which is saying something in and of itself. It is a really important ministry for Winnipeg Presbytery." David Swan wrote a letter of gratitude to the Presbytery on behalf of Affirm. In his letter, he called the establishment of Rainbow Ministry "a courageous action that will be a sign to many of the unchurched in our community that the United Church truly wishes to live up to its promise to accept gays and lesbians in all areas of the church. We have lit a lamp that will shine in the darkness of loneliness, isolation and fear that still fill the hearts of many gay and lesbian Christians."

16

THE WORLD IS WATCHING

*With this faith, we will be able to hew out of the mountain of despair
a stone of hope.*

Martin Luther King, Jr.

One of Bill Phipps' first acts as Moderator after he was elected at the 1997
General Council was to invite the gathering to join him in a song. He prefaced the song by saying that this year marks some very significant anniversaries: the end of the Ecumenical Decade of Churches in Solidarity with
Women, the anniversary of the church's apology to its aboriginal congregations, and the tenth anniversary of the church's decision to include gays and
lesbians in ministry. He reminded the Council that "we're not there yet."
There is much more work to be done on all these issues. He urged the
church to continue to work for justice. Then 600 people from all across The
United Church of Canada stood to join him in song. The song was written
by Holly Near when Harvey Milk, a gay city councillor from San Francisco,
was murdered. "We are a land of many colours..." sing the commissioners.
"We are a justice seeking people ... we are gay and straight together ... and
we are singing, singing for our lives."

Shortly after the 1988 decision, a United Church staff person was travelling by plane. She usually didn't make a point of talking about her
work, but when the person beside her asked what she did, she said
that she worked for the United Church. "Thank you," said the stranger.
"Thank you that your church has taken the discussion of homosexuality
out of the gutter and placed it around the dining room table." A lot of

people were watching the United Church and its debate, and for many of them, what one church said made an enormous difference.

For Bob Birney, a United Church lay person, the 1988 decision not to exclude gays and lesbians from ministry was a source of great hope. He grew up in the church and has been involved for many years in Affirm. He was one of its co-chairs for several years. He has also been a church musician in congregations. Growing up gay in a conservative family and society was very difficult. "I had a lot of problems with coming to terms with myself and accepting myself as a gay person," he says. "Before 1988 people wouldn't dream of mentioning homosexuality. We couldn't even face the concept. That's part of what made growing up so hard. There were just no role models."

Birney was still struggling with his own sense of the self at the time of the debate in the United Church. He found the years and months leading up to the 1988 decision extremely difficult. "I was totally stressed over the whole thing," he recalls. "It wasn't affecting my job since I didn't work for the church, but it was affecting who I was." He continues, the passion evident in his voice, "It was about my right to exist!" He felt that the positive decision gave him some sort of personal validation. It gave him a sense there was still room for him in the church, in the world. "It may well have contributed to my still being here," he says simply. "Faith is part of why one sticks around. Or at least it was for me." Maybe he'd have found a way to survive anyway, who knows? Birney is sure, however, that The United Church of Canada decision was a significant factor.

Dennis Stimson is a member of Parents and Friends of Lesbians and Gays. He has two sons, both now young men, both gay. "A person's sexuality is what God gave them. God made our children the way they are," he says emphatically, "and our God doesn't make mistakes!" He thinks the decision the United Church made around homosexuality and ministry gave a very positive message to gays and lesbians and their families. "The United Church said, in taking this approach, that gays and lesbians are human beings and not the outcasts of society. There are still many doors that are closed. The opening of this door is a very positive step." He thinks that what the church says still matters in society. "Even when you look at dwindling numbers and all that, the church still carries a lot of influence. A major step like the United Church took can have a lot of power. People look at it and say, 'Listen, this is what the United Church has done and the church hasn't collapsed.'" He thinks that kind of decision can even change attitudes. "People would hear all the arguments pro and con. They'd see that people they respected really studied and waded into it. Those decisions would carry weight, especially with people who were ambivalent." He thinks it has a kind of snowball effect: "The more you bring on line, the more will come on line."

John Fisher is the executive director of EGALE (Equality for Gays and Lesbians Everywhere), a national organization to promote gay and lesbian rights in Canada. He welcomes the changes in the United Church, believing that it does make a difference. He cautions the church against becoming too self-congratulatory, however, pointing out that for most of its history the church has been at the forefront of oppression against gays and lesbians. He points to the untold damage that has been done to gay and lesbian people by a consistently negative message from religious organizations about who they are and whether or not they even have the right to exist. "We believe church organizations have a responsibility to recognize the discrimination that they have been a part of in the past," Fisher says. "They're not just being nice when they make positive policy moves. They are undoing some of the damage that they have been a part of creating in the first place. It's not just a nice thing to do. It's an act of social responsibility." He notes that even now, virtually all the opposition to human rights legislation and same-sex benefits for gays and lesbians comes from religious communities. "Most of those who oppose this legislation are from the right-wing churches. So it is really important to have a voice of support, a dissenting voice, from the more moderate churches."

Ted Bingham now lives in Victoria, but he's originally from Halifax, where his father was a navy chaplain and Baptist minister. He's now 37 and although he has known about his own sexual orientation for many years, it's only in the last five years that he has really begun to come to terms with it. The United Church attracted him because it was more open than the Baptist church he was attending. "I joined because I saw it as a place that would welcome me as a gay person, though of course I know what the United Church decided in '88 is not what every United Church person believes. I think [the 1988 descision] attracted me because at least there was an official openness to gay people to enter in and be a part of the church. I think what happens with a lot of gay people is they don't think any church would want them at all. I remember when I first came out one of my worst fears was that this might mean I had to give up my faith. I felt like I would lose everything. Now I think it's silly that I ever thought that, but five years ago it was very real."

Bingham can sympathize with people who've been taught homosexuality is evil and wrong. He knows it takes time to work through that. "It took a long time for me to come to the conclusion that there's nothing wrong with me—no, I'm not sick. I'm OK." Some people know about his sexual orientation. "You pick and choose," he says. He is now ready to have his name used publicly. A few years ago he wrote a letter but didn't sign it because, as he puts it, "I just wasn't ready at that point. One of these days I have to put my name to something!" Both Bingham's parents died recently. One of his biggest regrets is that he never told them about his sexual orientation. "I struggled with telling them, but they were in their seventies and I thought, 'Why, at this point in their lives?' And yet there are days when I wonder. I was there when my mother died, and she looked at me—I felt that somehow she just knew anyway. My mother was taught from day one that this was wrong, so she might have thought about it and not voiced it, just letting it slip to the back of her mind."

The whole process of coming out has been very difficult at times, but also very freeing for Bingham. "I got myself so worked up. There were some Baptist friends that I came out to. I was scared out of my mind, but they've been amazingly supportive. It turned out that they'd known for a year or so anyway. When I finally got it said, one of them exclaimed, 'Is that all? I thought you were dying!'"

The Rev. Elizabeth Graham also is looking for a church home that can give some positive messages about homosexuality, to help undo some of the past hurt she and her family have experienced. She is applying to enter the United Church from another denomination. For her, it's not just about gays and lesbians in ministry, it's about offering welcome and acceptance to all. "The United Church has room for a wider selection of theologies," she explains. She feels there is room in the United Church for a range of different opinions on the issue of homosexuality—people who think it's sinful as well as gays and lesbians and their families. No one is told they must leave.

"One of the main things that made me decide to leave my own denomination was that it felt as though my own church was trying to get gays and lesbians out of the church. My daughter is lesbian and she was teaching Sunday school. It was suggested that gays and lesbians should not have any position of leadership within our congregation, not even singing in the choir, not teaching Sunday school. So she stopped teaching Sunday school." At the time, Graham was one of the ministers in her daughter's church. She found it extremely painful to leave her house on Sunday morning and leave her daughter behind, a daughter who as a young adult had been so active in the congregation. It still makes her angry. "You don't mess with my kids!" she says, "If it were only me, I could stay and be a thorn in their sides. But it's me and it's my brother and it's my daughter and it's my grandfather. I'm not just going to stick around. People have to take a stand. My daughter publicly stood up and told her story to the congregation. She started to cry. This really hurt her. And no one said a word to support her."

It may come as a surprise to many United Church congregations to realize how important a message they give when they say, explicitly or implicitly, "all are welcome here." Often they may not be aware that the person sitting beside them in the pew is soaking up that voice of love and welcome after years of hurt. "Kim" still lives a fairly closeted life. Although she doesn't hide her relationship, it isn't really acknowledged in the congregation. Even so, she knows she's in a safe place. Although some members express negative opinions about homosexuality, over all in the congregation there is what she describes as a "nearly palpable openness to trying new things and a reluctance to pass judgement." There is room for her.

Kim was involved with a charismatic Protestant church in her teens. In her twenties, she headed off to the mission field with an interdenominational organization. To her horror, she found herself in love with a fellow missionary—another woman! "This was a first for me," she says. "I was in shock, and yet thrilled by the remarkable intimacy we were discovering." The two women agonized and prayed, and finally, unable to bear the sense of self-condemnation any longer, they confessed their attraction to their leader. The two were separated, stripped of responsibility, and put through an improvised rehabilitation program for about six months. Finally they were reinstated, in separate countries.

Kim stayed with the organization for several more years, and returned to Canada thinking she had been "successfully heterosexualized." She was shaken to the core when she once more fell in love with a woman. "I felt God had broken a promise to me never to let this happen to me again. I felt I had done everything in my power to go straight, including pursuing several serious relationships with Christian men. I felt myself to be a huge hypocrite and a failure." Eventually she decided to give in completely to the feelings she had for women, "deciding that if I had to go to hell for love, I would." She left the church. In her personal life she felt happy and fulfilled, but felt that "if the truth were known, I would be a pariah in the eyes of most Christians." She still prayed, rather desperately and fearfully. She wasn't really sure if God was listening.

Some years later, Kim and her partner started to attend a United Church. Slowly, she started to rebuild her relationship with the church and with God. "It took me years of hearing sermons and conversations where gays and lesbians were viewed as manifestations of God's creative and ingenious diversity rather than as rebels and deviants to help heal my self-image and let me accept and celebrate myself again," she says. It was very important for her to be able to come out to her minister, several members of the congregation and her family and friends.

She feels safe in the church now, at long last. This sense of security and belonging is all the more important because she is losing a number of dear friends of a more fundamentalist persuasion. On the other hand, she feels she has gained new closeness with those church members who know and respect her for who she really is. And, what is more, she has regained her sense of personal integrity. "I am immensely grateful to those in the United Church who appreciate rather than revile people like me." she says. "Without them I would not have a church home, nor, in all likelihood, would I have peace in my relationship with God." There are countless other stories like these in the United Church of people who have regained a sense of faith and church community all because of the United Church's policy that all people, regardless of sexual orientation, can be members and ministers. But the decision didn't just affect individuals. It had an impact on the whole of Canadian society.

When Svend Robinson came out in 1988, it was a huge national story. Nowadays it's more commonplace. Vancouver itself has the largest number of gay and lesbian elected people in the world. In the last provincial election, all the candidates for all the major parties in the Vancouver-Burrard riding were lesbian or gay. It simply wasn't an issue. There was barely a word, even in the French media, when Réal Ménard, MP for Hochelaga-Maisonneuve, came out in 1994. It wasn't always that way.

Robinson grew up in the United Church. His mother had been a United Church member. He sang in the choir of Vancouver Heights United. "Some people say the United Church is the NDP at prayer," he remarks with a grin. He went to the 1988 General Council as an observer. "To witness the tremendous courage and eloquence of many people, gay or lesbian and straight, who spoke during that debate was for me really moving and inspirational," he says. He thinks the whole debate was very significant because this was the first mainstream church in Canada that was prepared to take a step towards equality. "It was important for the church but it was important beyond the church, because the struggles that took place had some very significant repercussions, particularly in smaller communities."

The church is often a very significant social institution in smaller communities. By bringing the discussion there, people had to struggle at a very personal level with an issue that previously had only been visible or discussed in big cities. But now, their friends, their neighbours, their family members were taking stands and talking about sexuality. Robinson notes that this discussion involved a lot of emotion—pain, sometimes anger. "It touched some of those communities to the core and it forced them to confront the issue. Invisibility and silence have historically been two of the greatest barriers to equality and justice for our gay and lesbian communities. The United Church, by engaging the debate, helped to break that silence and make that struggle visible. And as a result, people made the tremendously brave decision to move the discussion beyond the abstract, to say 'Just a minute, you're not talking about them; this is me, this is my life that you're talking about.'" Which is exactly what Robinson did when he came out in 1988.

Bill Siksay thinks the whole debate changed Canadian society even more than it changed the church. "It was a very positive step for gay and lesbian people in that it undercut the argument that Christianity was opposed to our legitimacy and that that there was a universal anti-gay theological position." Siksay thinks that 1984 was the real turning point and that what happened that year in the United Church was possibly even more significant than the final outcome in 1988.

In 1984 the report "Sexual Orientation and Eligibility for the Order of Ministry" went to General Council. Although its conclusions were not accepted in 1984, the report recommended that gays and lesbians be admitted into ministry in the United Church. Siksay thinks that one report made an enormous contribution to the secular political debate around human rights for gay and lesbian people. "The report that was produced in 1984 was the most significant gay and lesbian liberation document in Canadian history," he says. "It remains the most widely circulated gay and lesbian positive document ever published in Canada. It was such a controversial and unusual thing that I believe people read it." Even if they didn't read it, United Church people in virtually every community across Canada at least looked at it and knew that it was saying something positive. "Whether they agreed with it or not, that's got to have some kind of impact," Siksay says. He believes it was a significant opening for gay and lesbian people. "The publishing of the report in the *Observer* paved the way for a lot of things, including Svend Robinson's coming out in 1988. It was more possible because we'd done that work on a national level." The United Church often has acted out of a belief that it should and can have an impact on the world around it. The effect of what it did in 1988 is still being felt.

17

The Church in the World

---

*If we make our goal to live a life of compassion and unconditional
love, then the world will indeed become a garden where all kinds of
flowers can bloom and grow.*

Elizabeth Kubler-Ross

"An impossibly blue sky, a surge of warmth to ease a bitter winter, the birds at the feeder singing to the sun. My partner and I did our good deed for the day: our regular trip to the Red Cross to give the gift of life. I was told that my donation was going straight to the neo-natal ward of our largest city hospital. I felt terrific.

"And then I saw it. My car was still covered with last night's snow fall, and there on the windshield was the word 'fuk.' I rolled my eyes, for the spelling confirmed my suspicions about those who feel a need to write in the snow. Across the hood of the car was the word 'you.' At least they could spell that one. But in small letters, under the 'you,' was the clincher: 'homo.'

"My day took an about-face. Was it some neighbour kid (or worse, some neighbour adult) who, although they couldn't spell, did have the capacity to put two and two together? Was it a random act of meanness by someone whose worst insult was 'homo'? Was it the beginning of further acts of vandalism and violence? Would the writing in the snow be followed by spray paint, broken windows, verbal taunts, violence? Would our dogs be poisoned? Would we be safe in our own home?

"As the months have passed, my fears have faded. But the lesson hasn't. The lesson is that, no matter how good we are, no matter how neat we keep our homes, no matter how much we contribute to our community, there will still be those who deem us The Other. There will still be those who impress their friends by bullying The Other. There will still be those who really believe that their behaviour toward The Other is completely justified—and rational.

"In the big scheme of things, it hasn't mattered. There have been no further furtive messages of hate. No vandalism. No verbal taunts or physical violence. The dogs still frolic in the yard. No big deal. Except that—although the snow melted away that day—the message didn't."

🍎

On June 30, days before the celebration of Gay and Lesbian Pride Day in Saskatoon, an ad appeared in *The StarPhoenix* newspaper. In a large rectangle it had a picture of two stick figures, presumably male, holding hands. They were drawn in a red circle, with a line through them. Underneath was a list of passages from scripture: Romans 1; 1Corinthians 6:9-10; Leviticus 18:22; and Leviticus 20:13—the passage that recommends death by stoning as a penalty for homosexual relations. And beneath that a phone number where you could order a bumper sticker version for your car. Such an ad might well be written off as one person's opinion, but for the Leviticus passage, but for the fact that such attitudes all too often translate into real acts of violent hatred against people who are perceived to be lesbian or gay. Many police departments now have special units set up to deal with hate crimes. The Metropolitan Toronto Police Services defines a hate crime as "a criminal offence committed against a person or property that is based solely on the victim's race, religion, nationality, ethnic origin, gender, sexual orientation, or disability."

According to a 1995 report by Julien Roberts for the Canadian Department of Justice, there are about 60,000 hate crimes committed each year in Canada, of which approximately 10 per cent are directed against people perceived to be homosexual. The report also points out that "crimes of hate directed against the gay community are more likely to involve violence, or the threat of violence, than hate crimes directed against other groups." A 1995 study carried out by the 519 Church Street Community Centre in Toronto confirms this. It found that nearly 80 per cent of gay and lesbian respondents had experienced some form of verbal harassment. Over 30 per cent had been threatened by violence. Thirty per cent had been chased or followed. Over 16 per cent had been physically assaulted—beaten or punched, sometimes severely, usually by complete strangers. No wonder lesbians and gay men are fearful when threatening words appear on their car windshield.

No wonder some United Church people decided to speak up in protest against the ad in *The StarPhoenix*. Two days after the ad appeared, a hundred or so people showed up outside the offices of the newspaper. Many of them were United Church, from eight or nine different congregations in the city. On the way, one woman stopped to load her purse with buttons that said "The United Church of Canada supports lesbian, gay and bisexual people." She handed them out to the protesters. Lots of people wore them, whether they were the United Church or not. As for *The StarPhoenix*, the newspaper decided it didn't really need this kind of hassle, and decided to withdraw the ad.

Since the mid-1960s, in small ways and large, the United Church has been expressing its concern about the need to protect gay and lesbian people from violence and discrimination. In 1960, even though the United Church considered homosexuality a "sin" it still appealed to the federal government to decriminalize it. In 1969 homosexual activity in private between consenting adults was removed from the Criminal Code by then-Justice Minister Pierre Elliott Trudeau. Homosexuality was no longer a crime. Since then there have been fundamental changes in Canadian legislation.

In 1976 homosexuals were no longer barred as immigrants to Canada. By 1994 it was permissible, in certain circumstances, for lesbians and gays to sponsor same-sex partners to come to Canada. In 1976 Quebec became the first jurisdiction in Canada to prohibit discrimination on the basis of sexual orientation. By January 1998, all other jurisdictions except Prince Edward Island, Alberta and the Northwest Territories had included protection of gays and lesbians in their human rights legislation. An April 1998 ruling by the Supreme Court of Canada included sexual orientation as a prohibited grounds of descrimination in Alberta's human rights legislation. It is expected that the ruling will have a similar effect for Prince Edward Island and the Northwest Territories.

The United Church consistently has supported these changes. Its role has been two-fold, to engender non-discriminatory attitudes in society and to work for change in situations in which discrimination occurs. In 1975 John Damien was fired by the Ontario Racing Commission because he was a homosexual. He sued, in a much-publicized case that lasted 11 years. The United Church of Canada responded with support. In 1977 the United Church first began calling for changes to the Canadian Human Rights Act. "We affirm the right of persons, regardless of sexual orientation, to employment, accommodation, and access to services and facilities," said the church's Division of Mission in Canada in a submission regarding the act.

In May 1996, The United Church of Canada was called as a witness before the House of Commons Human Rights Committee. This was the committee dealing with Bill C-33, a bill to include sexual orientation as a prohibited ground of discrimination in the Canadian Human Rights Act.

The introduction of the bill had been welcomed warmly in a press release by then-Moderator Marion Best. Most witnesses strongly supported the bill. B'Nai Brith and the Canadian Jewish Congress argued that if one minority is vulnerable to discrimination other minorities are similarly at risk. The history of discrimination against Jewish people often has gone hand in hand with the victimization of homosexuals. There was some opposition to the bill, particularly from religious groups such as the Canadian Conference of Catholic Bishops and The Evangelical Fellowship of Canada.

In its presentation the United Church said that its own experience had taught the church that debates on the issue of sexual orientation can occur in a context of respect for different positions, can lead to principled decisions being made on a commitment of justice and love for all, and can result in a more inclusive community where healing of past divisions can occur and the total community becomes healthier and more enriched.

A member of the Commons Committee, MP Sheila Finestone, commented that she had followed The United Church of Canada discussions over the years with great interest. Finestone spoke in glowing terms of the United Church's record and consistency on human rights issues for gays and lesbians. She praised the United Church for its role, as she remembered with appreciation its participation in public hearings in 1985 when the Equality Rights Section of the Constitution was under discussion. The United Church's input had not gone unnoticed.

The United Church is now working on yet another area of change. The 1997 General Council endorsed a call for amendments to the federal Income Tax Act so that it treats same-gender partners the same as spouses. The act only permits spouses of the opposite sex to receive spousal pension plan benefits. The proposed changes are consistent with a 1992 General Council decision to extend benefits to same-sex partners of all church employees.

It's hard to measure how much impact things like resolutions, briefs and presentations can make. Bill Doyle thinks they make a difference. He is a lawyer and, as an out gay man, a substantial portion of his practice is from gay and lesbian people. Doyle considers himself fortunate to be self-employed. He figures he takes far too much time off for church and volunteer work, but on the other hand, "that's what keeps me going on a day-to-day basis," he says. He's on a lot of church committees. Locally he is the co-chair of the Manitoba Conference Sexism Committee. He has been a presbytery representative, and a member of Affirm. Lately, he's the United Church's representative to the Inter-church Committee for Refugees and the co-chair of the Division of Mission in Canada (DMC) Church in Society Co-ordinating Committee. For five years he has been a member of a DMC committee dealing with human rights concerns—women, human rights, racism, gender and sexual orientation.

Through that committee Doyle was part of the process to support the amendment to the Canadian Human Rights Act and also the hate crimes legislation (an amendment to the criminal code to include sexual orientation in the hate crimes section). On one occasion Doyle was at a meeting with Allan Rock, who was at that time the Minister of Justice. He recalls the Justice Minister telling him how important it was to have church groups on side so that the government had visible support. "He saw it as a necessary condition for the changes to be made, because it was seen publicly as a real hot potato," Doyle recalls. "They didn't want to take any political hits because of it. Allan Rock mentioned the need for the United Church support—they needed as much support as they could garner to take the heat off themselves." Doyle wonders if "they only changed the legislation because they were forced to—really they didn't want to touch it. The United Church did have an impact."

Doyle is now quite open about his sexual orientation in his work and personal life, and in the church. That's a change for him. "With the greater involvement that the United Church has taken in a lot of gay and lesbian human rights issues, there appears to have been greater opportunity for gay and lesbian people to share their gifts with the church," he says. He believes that the changes within the church have gone hand in hand with the church's work in the world to protect the human rights of gays and lesbians.

The United Church may not have changed the world overnight. Doyle knows that any changes tend to be incremental. But the church has made a difference for the lives of gay and lesbian people. "Having the United Church behind a minority group gives the issue and the group some credibility, or even maybe just a louder voice," he says. Doyle thinks that the wider society is aware of the position that the United Church has taken, and it may have changed the way they view the church. "People within the gay and lesbian community have long stereotyped the church as being an unfriendly place for them. With the stand that the United Church has taken publicly they can no longer characterize the churches right across the board that way. They have to acknowledge that the church has taken some steps in solidarity with them," he says.

Barry Deeprose is president of Ottawa's Pink Triangle Services, an organization that provides advocacy, education and support for gays and lesbians. He also has been a volunteer on the gay line for the past 18 years. Deeprose has heard a lot of stories. He thinks the role of the church is important, and that it needs to be doing more. "There is a great need in the gay and lesbian community for acknowledgement of the spiritual aspect of our lives," he says. "There is an enormous need to see the church is committed to gay and lesbian issues. That sort of affirmation is really important. People coming out need to hear those voices."

Deeprose would like to see the churches, all churches, give a message that gays and lesbians are not just tolerated, but actively embraced as part of the church community church. He imagines the churches all coming out on Gay Pride Day to show their support, or a whole list of churches that are committed to supporting Pride Day printed in the daily newspaper. "It would make a lot of people feel really good to see something like that in the *Ottawa Citizen*." Pride Days are a very important symbol for many gay and lesbian people, he explains. "We are brought up with a feeling of shame. The opposite of that is gay pride. By being visible we unlearn what we have learned. Until we can get out and walk in the sunshine, we still live with that shame. People in congregations need to hear this, people coming out have to hear this from outside themselves and outside the community. Churches have to come out of the closet a bit and declare their support openly." Sometimes that happens, even in places like British Columbia's Okanagan Valley.

It's June 28, 1997. About 400 people have shown up for Gay and Lesbian Pride Day in Kelowna. The hour-long parade wends its way through the Kelowna City Park along the edge of Lake Okanagan, past sunbathers, sidewalk vendors, a rugby tournament and an assortment of spectators. It's a small community, so people know one another. Aside from one lone drag queen, most of the marchers could blend back easily into the small businesses, fruit orchards, campuses and churches from whence they came. There are a number of United Church people in the parade, including three United Church ministers, showing their support.

One of the United Church people is Ray McGinnis. He works as an educator at Naramata Centre, a United Church educational centre in the nearby village of Naramata. He was invited to be a grand marshall for the Pride '97 parade. Organizers asked him to speak as an openly gay man and as a person involved in the church. "I am glad to be a member of a church which has affirmed its acceptance of all human beings as persons made in the image of God regardless of their sexual orientation," McGinnis begins. There is much applause. "In our Western culture, sexuality and spirituality have been separated from each other. Homophobia in our culture has threatened the ability of the gay and lesbian community to say yes to your sexuality and yes to our Creator." More applause. "Anyone can say 'I believe in God.' Too often people who say they believe most strongly in God have not believed that God loves and accepts gay and lesbian people. I do. The God I trust loves unconditionally. I trust in a God who says 'no' to violence against lesbians and gays, and says 'yes' to hospitality and justice for all." McGinnis is the only person to speak about God that day, the only person to "come out" as a Christian. Afterwards, several people not connected with the church come up to tell him how glad they are to see the United Church "walking the talk."

The parade has dispersed. People in the park are jogging, strolling along eating cotton candy, playing Frisbee, having picnics. McGinnis prepares to return to Naramata Centre to begin training staff for the summer programs. Things have returned to normal, yet something has changed. People used to hearing words of condemnation from the church have heard words of support. Something also has shifted for McGinnis. "I took a step away from fear," he says. "And most of the people who witnessed this small step embraced and cheered me on. I don't know if there is more love and acceptance in the world. I do know that my conscious intention to ask for support and to trust that God would be with me in all this has given me more courage to keep on living my life."

18

Daring to Be United

For all that has been—thanks! For all that shall be—Yes!

Dag Hammarskjold

El camino se hace al andar. (We make the way by walking.)

Chilean saying

It's Pride Day in Toronto. In extravagant and sometimes outrageous ways, a marginalized community proclaims its presence. Sometimes there's an in-your-face defiance: "You may not like us but we're here to stay!" Mostly, though, the mood is festive and joyful. An 81-year-old woman has decided to march in the parade this year. She is there because her congregation, Glen Rhodes United, just recently became an Affirming Congregation and she wants to be supportive. She has never been to Pride Day before, and yet there she is. There are other people from her church at the parade as well who also have never been to such an event before. Whenever the parade stops, she dances. The crowd of onlookers cheers enthusiastically at the sight of an old woman dancing with uninhibited joy. At the end of parade she is still there, and she's still dancing.

T he United Church has changed over the last 10 years, in its policy, its attitudes, its theology, and its practice. Inevitably, other denomina tions around the world have been forced to face their own Issue Years. Many of them look to the United Church for models and ways to get through. They look at how far we have come, and they ask us how we did it.

The process of change in The United Church of Canada is not over, nor would anyone say the church has "arrived," but there are many signs the church is a very different place than it was in 1988. At that time, most people believed it would be a decade or more before even one congregation would accept an openly lesbian or gay minister. Since then, seven openly lesbian or gay candidates have been settled in pastoral charges. Many more clergy have been called as openly gay or lesbian, or have subsequently come out to their congregations. Nine congregations have made public statements declaring themselves to be affirming and welcoming of lesbians and gays in all aspects of their congregational life, including ministry. Many more are reflecting more quietly on ways their congregation might offer a more inclusive welcome to all regardless of sexual orientation.

Like all major denominations in Canada, the United Church still struggles with declining membership and increasingly limited finances. But there are many signs that it is still a strong, healthy church, offering spiritual nurture to some three million Canadians, and a life-giving and caring presence in 4,000 communities across the country. There is no question that the United Church lost members because of the issue—best estimates place the losses at 25,000—but it also gained members. In some places it also acquired a new sense of its mission and a whole new vitality.

The real costs and gains of the United Church's 1988 decision are in many ways immeasurable. There was no way the United Church could have faced the issue of ministry and homosexuality and come out unscathed. Whatever it decided, it would have lost members. If it had chosen, as some people thought it should, to completely bar lesbians and gays from ministry, it might have lost the skills and resources of at least 10 per cent of its clergy and members, as well as many friends, family members and supporters of lesbians and gays. Even in its compromise decision, the church lost people from both sides who were unwilling to live with its uneasy ambiguity.

The United Church always has been a diverse institution. Its carefully crafted founding charter, the Basis of Union, reflects the delicate balancing act required to forge a single institution out of its founding denominations. Diversity of its membership and of its belief always has characterized the United Church. In its attempts to create space for divergent opinion, life experience and faith, it sometimes has been accused of being wishy-washy, of not knowing what it really believes. Yet diversity has been one of the United Church's greatest strengths—its ability to preach God's word without insisting that everyone believe the same thing, its ability to take stands on social issues while continuing to respect those voices that disagree. Maintaining diversity is perhaps the United Church's biggest accomplishment out of The Issue years. It is still a church that holds together, hangs together, argues together. It is a church where you can find, on any given Sunday, and even sometimes side-by-side in the same pew, gays and lesbians who are open and comfortable about their sexuality and people who think homosexuals are unrepentant sinners. It is a church that says all are welcome, regardless of their sexual orientation, regardless of their opinion about sexual orientation. It is still a church that dares to be united and uniting across the full spectrum of human experience. But getting there has not been easy.

There are some who fought bitterly against including lesbians and gays in any way in the church. And there are some who fought just as bitterly against putting up barriers, not always because they approved of homosexuality, sometimes just because it's not very United Church to shut people out. Many people were very angry. Some left. Sometimes those confrontations left a bitter legacy. It took a long time for people to start feeling good again about being the United Church.

Generally, United Church people don't like extremism, and they don't like people attacking one another personally. As the more vitriolic feelings died down, many people felt sad and a bit disappointed that the church had slipped into such a morass. That wasn't how they wanted to be as a community of faith, whatever their position on this particular issue.

For many years people noticed a weariness, and a caution, about justice issues—any issues. It was as though, having gone through such terrible conflict, people didn't want to risk getting into arguments about anything else. It took a good 10 years for the shock to begin to wear off. "The church is no longer feeling shell-shocked," says Bill Siksay. He has hung in with the church, even if at times he felt a little shell-shocked himself. "The intensity of the debate and division is gone from the congregational life of the church," he feels. "The church seems generally very positive about the place of gays and lesbians in the church. It's just not that much of an issue any more. People who were skeptical are less skeptical now. I see people wanting to celebrate being the church again."

When Bill Phipps was elected Moderator of the United Church in the summer of 1997, people were prepared for a bit of controversy. He was well-known for his outspoken advocacy on justice issues—aboriginal rights and land claims, poverty, economics, human rights and the rights of gays and lesbians. But the first issue to land him on the front pages of national newspapers was what he said about faith. In a free-wheeling, hour-and-a-half discussion with him, the *Ottawa Citizen* asked what his personal beliefs were about Jesus, heaven and hell, and the resurrection. Phipps was his usual direct, frank self. The *Citizen* then reported that he didn't believe Jesus was God and didn't believe Jesus rose from the dead as a "scientific fact." Later, when Phipps elaborated on those cryptic summaries, he said, "Jesus embodies as much of the nature of God as you can embody in a human being. I see Jesus as coming from God, revealing part of the nature of God. But he did not reveal all of God ... There is no question that Jesus is at the centre of my life and faith. Jesus represents what God wants us to do and be." There was an immediate response, from those who supported him and those who disagreed with his remarks.

Phipps is not the first United Church Moderator to make the headlines with controversial statements about faith. Dr. Bob McClure, Moderator from 1968-'71, said he regarded Jesus "as a son of man so much more than emphasizing he is the son of God" and the fur flew then! In a 1988 *Observer* survey two thirds of United Church members surveyed said they didn't believe Jesus was the only way to God. Fifty-one per cent of them said they didn't believe in hell.

The United Church never has required, or maintained, unanimity amongst its members. Some people applauded Phipps' comments as a breath of fresh air, while others worried once again about what the United Church was up to. Some were quite delighted with the interest the secular world was showing, pleased about this new opportunity to have a public debate on issues of faith and spirituality. Others wondered aloud whether Jesus really cared so much about what people believed as about how they treated one another. The United Church, in all its diversity, has not lost its fighting spirit.

In the midst of the furor over Jesus, Phipps' opinions about homosexuality and his strong support for gay and lesbian ministers largely went unnoticed. Maybe it really isn't so much of an issue for the church anymore. Phipps thinks that's the case. "It seems to be a non-topic of conversation," he says. "Congregations can clearly flourish with gay and lesbian leadership. There was a great fear that congregations would disintegrate, and that's simply not true." He personally wouldn't be surprised if the majority of United Church people still disagree with the United Church decision, but "the church hasn't fallen apart. Their congregation is still going along fine."

Phipps understands why there's still some reluctance to get into big heavy issues again. "It's like when you have a conflict with a person you love. You work your way through it and somehow or another you come out of it. Both of you have gained some understanding and both of you have moved. You didn't solve everything, but you don't go back at it right away. You have to give it some time to live with it. And that's what we've been doing as a church."

Phipps looks back on those years of The Issue with mixed emotions. He recalls all the tears and anger and shouting and arms around each other, the weeping and gnashing of teeth. "We've been awfully tame in the church over the past 10 years," he reflects. "Sometimes I wish there were a little more anger or tears. I'd like to see people getting a little more of that kind of energy for something like economic justice, for example. I have seen the intensity of what debating this does to people. And how it can tear people apart. We did some awful stuff to each other, but I've also seen people being changed. I think that in those years, in all that intensity, people had to grow in ways they did not want to grow. They had to learn something new." But it was painful, as change so often is, and for awhile the church seemed to collectively retreat a bit.

The church had a lot of collective healing to do, Phipps says, and that takes time. He thinks that now, a decade or so later, it's time to emerge. "We're beginning to stick our heads up over our blankets and say 'We've got to be out in the world.' The issues that I think we've got to be taking on have to do with poverty, racism, aboriginal people, economic, racial and environmental injustices. And if we can do that, by God, we will find ourselves standing shoulder-to-shoulder in that struggle with a woman minister we may not have accepted 20 years ago and a gay minister whom we didn't accept 10 years ago. But we're together with our gospel taking on issues of injustice. And gay and lesbian people, and all other kinds of people will be just working in the church like everyone else as we do our prophetic work together."

Bob Smith was Moderator from 1984-1986, through some of the stormy years of The Issue. "I think we were surprised at what it was possible for us to do," he says, "and I think we paid a very heavy price as a church. We said, 'We did it, we're glad we did it, but it hurt so bad we never want to do that again.' And yet I long for the church to be risking its life again. And I think we did. We really did."

Perhaps it will do so again, for the United Church is no stranger to risk or controversy. It was born out of a difficult and painful union. Through all its history it has spoken about and acted on social issues—from Japanese internment in World War II, to apartheid in South Africa, abortion, capital punishment, rights for women, human rights, refugees, native land claims, economic justice, child poverty and homosexuality. It often runs counter to popular opinion, and constantly strives to live with integrity with its own internal disagreements. That's just who the United Church is. It's not a denomination insulated from the world around it, and it refuses to stick its head in the sand. It changes, and it creates change. It is very far from perfect, as any United Church person would be the first to tell you. Yet it continues to risk talking about and living out what it believes, and, above all, it dares to be the church in the world.

Appendix A

Gift, Dilemma and Promise:
A Report and Affirmations on Human Sexuality
The United Church of Canada
1984

This report contains Affirmations on Sexuality and Selfhood; Marriage; Intimacy; Sexism, Society, Self; Sexual Orientation as approved by the 30th General Council. It is recommended that they be studied in the context of, and not apart from, Gift, Dilemma and Promise.

Sexuality and Selfhood
Acknowledgements and Affirmations

a. We affirm that our sexuality is a gift of God. In its life-enhancing, non-exploitive forms it is a primary way of relating to ourselves and to one another and is the way God has chosen to continue the human race.

> We acknowledge that human sexuality, like all other aspects of human nature, is affected and distorted by human sinfulness. We recognize the ambiguity of human nature and therefore of human sexuality. "All have sinned and fall short of the glory of God." (Romans 3:23)

b. We affirm that God works in Christ through the Spirit to redeem human nature and, with it, human sexuality. (cf Romans 8:21f)

c. We affirm that the giving and receiving of affection, whether physical or emotional or both, is a basic need.

> The forms which this may take are many and varied. Because the hunger for intimacy is ultimately a hunger for God, this is a profoundly spiritual experience. It may lead to a more profound humanness or to manipulation, distortion, control. We acknowledge that the roles and expectations that accompany gender are largely cultural in origin and arbitrary in nature.

d. We affirm that even in the midst of ambiguity, we are called upon to make responsible decisions with regard to the expression of our sexuality and to cope with the consequences.

> We need to "hear the pluralism and diversity of moral decision making within the church as a possible way in which God is engaging us," says one of the responses to the Human Sexuality Study.

e. We affirm the church's call to proclaim the worth of human sexuality and to speak out concerning the abuses of human sexuality in individual lives, in the community and in the structures of society. In this respect, we understand that our responsibility is more to challenge and support than to condemn, more prophetic and pastoral than imperial.

> We acknowledge that the way we experience and express our sexuality is shaped largely by the ways in which we are socialized, by our unique journeys through the stages of human development, and by our personal journey of faith.

f. We affirm the role of the church as a community of faith, offering support, challenge and guidance in sexual decision making.

g. We affirm that the church is called to a ministry of prophetic witness in the face of evil, pastoral care in the face of pain and confusion, education in the face of conflicting values and ignorance. This includes the ethical dimensions of: birth control and family planning, family life education, marriage preparation and enrichment, counselling in situations of marriage breakdown, separation and divorce, unfulfilling relationships, sexual exploitation in the family, sexism (personal and social discrimination against others on the basis of gender), concerns of singles, of unmarried couples, homosexual persons and single-parent families.

h. We affirm that the church is called to initiate and support research and educational programs to increase our understanding of the causes of exploitive sexual behaviour and other destructive expressions of sexuality, to reduce the incidence of such destructive expressions, and to improve our ministry to all who are harmed by such behaviour.

Marriage
Acknowledgements and Affirmations

a. We affirm that marriage is a gift of God through which Christians make a covenant with one another and with God.

In marriage we offer one another the promise of lifelong companionship, rich expression of human affections and sexuality, and nurture for the children. Marriage as an institution can undergird each relationship and provide stability for society.

We affirm the value of marriage and that the church must work both to redeem and care for the institution and to support those entering into a covenant relationship with each other.

We acknowledge that marriage can also be destructive. Marriage as an institution is shaped by cultural attitudes that are patriarchal and oppressive.

As an institution at the present time it more readily supports male supremacy than human equality, reflecting current values in society. It can degenerate into exploitation, abuse and violence, including rape.

Marriage is an instrument which shares in human sin and which may be redeemed by grace to become the vehicle God intended. It is not to be idealized or idolized as an end in itself.

b. We affirm that in Christian marriage a man and woman give themselves to each other in the full intention of a lifelong commitment.

Nothing less can measure its totality, even though they may fail in their best intentions and efforts.

In self-giving they become one, a new unity. Yet they do not own each other, as no human being may so possess another. They own the gifts of love and commitment and grace that each has freely offered.

This self-giving love over the years may lead into the most mature and complete joy in each other.

c. We affirm that this unity is a creation of God and is greater than the two individuals.

It creates holy ground on which the two, and all others, must walk carefully and gently, yet forthrightly and with courage. It has boundaries, between them and with others, that may not be trespassed. It takes precedence over other relationships. It calls for that caring which heals hurt and tends growth.

d. We affirm that sexual intercourse in marriage is intended to be:
  - a profound expression of the whole person;
  - a yearning for total union with the other;
  - a creative and holy expression of fulfillment in the other person.

  We acknowledge that:
  - sexual intercourse may be exploitive, using the other for one's gratification;

- it is possible to be genitally exclusive while not being genuinely faithful. Faithfulness cannot be contained in or reduced to sexual exclusivity, any more than covenant can be contained in or reduced to law.

e. We affirm that marriage from a Christian perspective is based on faithfulness expressed through:

- choosing each other above all others;

    This choosing has its greatest meaning when it is given and maintained gladly rather than as a grudging legalism.

- risking and being vulnerable in the relationship;

- The alternative is, in the long run, to retreat into alienation or two solitudes;

- willingness to put into the relationship the patience, understanding and the work required to help it grow;

- accepting and nurturing the other for his or her unique gifts; putting the other before one's own interests in a lifelong commitment which is spiritual, emotional and physical;

- and that these intentions are most fully achieved and symbolized when sexual intercourse in marriage is exclusive.

    Faithfulness of this kind is a spiritual gift to be received in the grace of God. It recognizes that when we fail, God is faithful still, and we may discover forgiveness and renewal.

f. We recognize the commitment that is present in many relationships other than Christian marriage; and that the church is called to minister to people in these relationships as in others.

g. We affirm that the church is called to emphasize and work for the essential values in marriage and family that contribute to the wholeness of persons and to challenge those forms and attitudes that limit and degrade personal worth, even when the culture supports them.

    These include the unjust social structures of patriarchy and sexism as well as distorted attitudes such as rigid role-stereotyping.

Intimacy
Acknowledgements and Affirmations

a. We affirm that God has made us with a longing to belong, to reach out to one another, to touch each other's lives as members one of another.

    Though we think and act as if we were individuals, in fact we are social beings, needing one another.

b. We affirm that all people experience hunger for intimacy that is a profoundly spiritual matter, a hunger for God. It is in our experience of the intimate God that we find the grace and possibility of intimacy with one another.

> God leads us
> - to treat the other as a person of equal value to oneself;
> - to respect the other's relationships with other people;
> - to be vulnerable to the changes, even the hurt, that may come from openness to another;
> - to commitment and patience as the relationship grows;
> - to the discovery of self more fully through experiencing the other;
> - to take seriously the dangers in intimacy and be careful to limit or prevent them;
> - to recognize our failures of intimacy and be willing to accept forgiveness.
>
> God is a God of loving kindness, patience, forgiveness...
>
> In risking intimacy we may glimpse God's grace...
>
> In being forgiven, learn to forgive...
>
> We acknowledge that there are many forms of intimacy; some are enriching; others are exploitive. The Bible offers many models to help us understand and express these. Ultimately, God is the most intimate and yet transcendent companion in life's journey of intimacy, and so the source and energy of all our seeking for each other.

c. We affirm the importance in intimate relationships of respecting the integrity of others, of setting limits on our actions.

> The Bible expresses this both in terms of responsible love and of guidelines or rules for behaviour.

d. We affirm singleness as a state in which people may find intimacy and fulfillment.

> We acknowledge that the church has too readily accepted marriage as the norm for society and so has not valued single persons for themselves or given them the place that is rightfully theirs, nor allowed them the opportunity of sexual fulfillment. Each person needs to struggle faithfully with these decisions.

e. We affirm that celibacy, freely chosen, can be an expression of God's will and can include emotional intimacy.

> We acknowledge that the church has not taken celibacy as a vocation with sufficient seriousness, and so has neither benefited fully from its riches nor provided the support it requires. Its value as a temporary or as a lifelong commitment needs further study.

f. We affirm that learning to express our longing for intimacy both lovingly and responsibly is a lifelong task as God calls us into full humanity.

Sexism, Society, Self
Acknowledgements and affirmations

a. We affirm that the intention of God for all persons is full equality in both our personal and social lives, including acceptance of our sexual differences and similarities.

b. We affirm that the essence of equality is the acceptance and appreciation of the gifts of all persons female and male.

> We acknowledge that all sexism in language, in social and economic structures, in the conventions of our society, and in the attitudes of individuals, is destructive to human dignity and opposed to the will of God.

c. We affirm that God calls us as a church to eliminate all forms of sexism (personal and social discrimination against others on the basis of gender) in the life and worship of the congregations, presbyteries, Conferences and national structures of The United Church of Canada, in keeping with guidelines established by the General Council of The United Church of Canada.

d. We affirm the need for ongoing research and action in relation to those aspects of life in which sexism (personal and social discrimination against others on the basis of gender) is commonly found.

e. We affirm that the traditional patriarchal structuring of society can be redeemed and eventually transformed through the grace of God and the struggles of those willing to face the contradictions of sexism. We affirm that Christians are called to work towards an inclusive society.

Sexual Orientation
Acknowledgements and Affirmations

a. We affirm our acceptance of all human beings as persons made in the image of God regardless of their sexual orientation.

> Accumulated social science research and the articulated experience of the vast majority of both heterosexual and homosexual men and women affirm that sexual orientation is not so much a matter of choice as a "given" aspect of one's identity resulting probably from a complex interaction of genetic and environmental factors.

b. We affirm salvation for all people is by grace through faith and that all believers in Christ are accepted as full members of the Christian church regardless of their sexual orientation.

> We acknowledge that the church has encouraged, condoned and tolerated the rejection and persecution of homosexual persons in society and in the church, and call it to repent.

c. We affirm that the church is called to initiate and encourage communication and discussion with homosexual believers about sexuality in order that fellowship may be increased and misunderstanding, fears and hostilities lessened.

> In learning more about sexual orientation the church can benefit from the input of the homosexual community which is working to articulate its own history, understanding of sexuality, and its relationship to the broader church and society.

d. We affirm that members of the church, individually and corporately, are responsible for becoming more aware of discrimination against homosexual persons, taking action to ensure that they enjoy their full civil and human rights in society, working to end all forms of discrimination against them, and for personally supporting the victims of such discrimination.

> In March 1977 the Department of Church in Society of the Division of Mission in Canada, passed the following resolution:
>
> "...We affirm the right of persons regardless of their sexual orientation to employment, accommodation, and access to the services and facilities that they need and desire.
>
> Recommendation: That in all areas covered by The Canadian Human Rights Act, provision should be made for prohibiting discrimination on the basis of 'sexual orientation.'"

e. We affirm the need, as the church engages its heterosexual and homosexual members in dialogue, to recognize the personal and professional risks to which homosexual persons open themselves as they respond to this invitation.

f. We affirm the need for all church members, both heterosexual and homosexual, to study and understand sexuality and lifestyles in the light of the gospel.

Appendix B

Membership, Ministry and Human Sexuality:
A New Statement of The United Church of Canada
by the 32nd General Council
1988

Council Re-affirmed...

quoting from the statement of the 30th General Council "Gift, Dilemma, & Promise," 1984:

a. We affirm that marriage is a gift of God through which Christians make a covenant with one another and with God.

b. We affirm that in Christian marriage a man and woman give themselves to each other in the full intention of a lifelong commitment.

c. We affirm that this unity is a creation of God and is greater than the two individuals.

d. We affirm that sexual intercourse in marriage is intended to be:
   - a profound expression of the whole person;
   - a yearning for total union with the other;
   - a creative and holy expression of fulfillment in the other person.

e. We affirm that marriage from a Christian perspective is based on faithfulness.

f. We recognize the commitment that is present in many relationships other than Christian marriage; and that the church is called to minister to people in these relationships, as in others.

g. We affirm that the church is called to emphasize and work for the essential values in marriage and family that contribute to the wholeness of persons and to challenge those forms and attitudes that limit and degrade personal worth, even when the culture supports them.

Council Confessed...

Of Faith

1. We confess that God is the Creator of the earth and all that is, including humanity in all its diversity.

2. We confess that God speaks authoritatively through the Old and New Testaments.

3. We confess that God's Spirit offers us comfort, healing, and support, and challenges us in ways we may experience as difficult and disturbing.

4. We confess our creation in the image of God and that as Christians we are called into covenant community as sisters and brothers in Christ.

Of Sin

5. We confess that we are a broken and hurting community. In our search for God's intention, at times we have become fractious and judgemental and have both caused and experienced hurt, misunderstanding, and estrangement.

6. We confess before God that as a Christian community, we have participated in a history of injustice and persecution against gay and lesbian persons in violation of the Gospel of Jesus Christ.

Of Infirmity

7. We confess our continued confusion and struggle to understand homosexuality, even as we confess our history of sinfulness.

8. We confess our inability at this time, given our diversity in our understanding of the authority and interpretation of scripture, to find consensus regarding a Christian understanding of human sexuality, including homosexuality.

Of Fact

9. We confess that we have not all responded to the acclamation of appreciation of the effective participation of our Christian gay and lesbian brothers and sisters in all aspects of our church's life, including the Order of Ministry, as declared at the 30th General Council.

10. We confess that only recently has The United Church of Canada become aware of and involved in the dialogue leading toward a Christian understanding of human sexuality.

In light of the foregoing confessional statement, the 32nd General Council challenges The United Church of Canada to continue to be a covenant community, wherein:

- we recognize that all have sinned and fallen short of God's intention for us;

- we agree that God's intention for all human relationships is that they be faithful, responsible, just, loving, health-giving, healing and sustaining of community and self;

- we acknowledge that we are unclear at the present time, as to what God's complete intention is in relation to human sexuality, even as we affirm our support and appreciation for the gifts of Christian marriage, the charism of celibacy, and the way of chaste singleness.

On the strength of our ongoing covenant relationship as The United Church of Canada, we are called to examine two theologically based but culturally conditioned views, namely:

- an undue emphasis on sexual morality which has, from time to time, caused the Christian church to lose perspective on the whole variety of human sinfulness; and,

- an undue elevation of the sexual aspect of our being, in our times, making this an idol which we worship.

Neither view is fully consistent with God's intention for us, nor has either view liberated us to faithful love in Christ.

Council Declared...

1. That all persons, regardless of their sexual orientation, who profess faith in Jesus Christ and obedience to Him, are welcome to be or become full members of The United Church of Canada.

2 a. All members of The United Church of Canada are eligible to be considered for ordered ministry.

   b. All Christian people are called to a lifestyle patterned on obedience to Jesus Christ.

   c. That all congregations, presbyteries, and Conferences covenant to work out the implications of sexual orientation and lifestyles in light of the Holy Scriptures, according to their responsibilities as stated in *The Manual*.

3. That the 32nd General Council affirm the present ordination/commissioning procedures as outlined in *The Manual*, and those actions taken at the 30th General Council, which state, it is inappropriate to ask about the sexual orientation of those in the candidacy process, or those in the call/appointment/settlement process.

4. That the report "Toward a Christian Understanding of Sexual Orientations, Lifestyles and Ministry" does not reflect the present position of The United Church of Canada; therefore this report ought to be considered an historic document and the decisions of the 32nd General Council be circulated for study and reflection in our struggle to find God's direction for our church.

Council Issued a Call...

To the Church:

5. That there be further church-wide study of the authority and the interpretation of scripture and the theological and cultural premises that inform our understanding.

6. That the 32nd General Council ask congregations, presbyteries, Conferences and the appropriate Divisions to respond to the call for further study and dialogue, related to the broad spectrum of sexual responsibility and continue to make available existing educational resources, including those of the ecumenical community.

7. That the 32nd General Council urge the appropriate Divisions and courts of the church to take action to address the church's participation in oppression of people on the basis of sexual orientation.

8. That the 32nd General Council through the appropriate Divisions and courts of the church address the issue of our concern for pastoral care of individuals and groups in our United Church of Canada community, who feel unheard, manipulated, or estranged.

To Society:

That, since within Canada, only Quebec, Manitoba, Ontario, and the Yukon Territory have human rights legislation that provides equal protection under the law from discrimination against gay and lesbian persons, but the human rights codes of the Government of Canada, the remaining provinces, and the Northwest Territories do not include such legislation, the 32nd General Council:

- urge all levels of government in Canada to guarantee and ensure that the human rights of their gay and lesbian inhabitants are fully protected by law;

- urge all courts, congregations and appropriate Divisions of The United Church of Canada to become active in support of human rights for lesbian and gay people;

- request the Division of Mission in Canada to make information, educational resources and study guides available to support pastoral charges, presbyteries and Conferences in these endeavours.

Having studied the petitions sent to it, the 32nd General Council also received the report, "Toward a Christian Understanding of Sexual Orientations, Lifestyles and Ministry," along with the Dissenting Statements (Parts 2 and 3 only), as fulfilling the mandate given by the 30th General Council, 1984.

Footnote:
For purposes of readability, the numbering system used during debate on the issue during General Council has been simplified. The action of the General Council on the original report has been moved to the end for purposes of clarity. The text of the Council's action remains the same.

Issued by the General Council Office, August 1988.

APPENDIX C

LET'S TALK ABOUT HOMOPHOBIA...
A resource developed and approved by
The Division of Ministry Personnel and Education
The United Church of Canada,
1990

Words spoken by some United Church folk...

"Most often when a face is attached to an issue, people can be reasonable and rational and even compassionate. The real horror for me in being found out is that I have known people's anger and fear against homosexual people to be such that they are not beyond brutally attacking gay and lesbian people. Living with that kind of fear eventually kills the soul."

...a faithful choir member

"While everyone else in the group took their turn lifting up something to celebrate about life with their spouse, I realized that I had much to celebrate about life with my partner, but that I wouldn't dare speak about it."

...a U. C. W. member

"I'm not sure how much longer I can live with the life and dilemma of remaining silent about my sexual orientation so that I may be accepted, and declaring myself so that I may be set free."

...a student in the candidature process

"One of the hardest things is when people on the one hand speak in absolutely glowing terms about what I'm like and what I'm doing

and then in the next breath rage about those 'sick perverts that ought to be lined up and shot.'"

...an ordained minister

"On being received as a member in The United Church of Canada where, 'You are entitled to all the rights and privileges of membership in The United Church of Canada.' For me there was a gut wrenching, knowing that this was not true."

...a new member of The United Church

A **phobia** is a "persistent and irrational fear of a specific object, activity or situation that results in a compelling desire to avoid the dreaded object, activity, or situation." *(American Psychiatric Association, 1980)*

Homophobia...

...is a pervasive irrational fear of homosexuality.

...more closely resembles a prejudice than a phobia.

...contains not only fear but an element of hatred.

...causes persons to avoid behaviours (particularly affectionate and expressive behaviours towards members of his/her own sex) that might be construed as "gay."

...causes heterosexual persons to fear any homosexual feelings within themselves.

AS A COMMUNITY WE MUST RECOGNIZE OUR HOMOPHOBIA AND TAKE RESPONSIBILITY FOR COUNTERACTING THE BIAS THAT RUNS THROUGH OUR CULTURE, OUR INSTITUTIONS, OUR CHURCH.

A Christian Response to Homophobia

Much of God's work of creation is filled with mystery. Human sexuality is one of those mysteries which causes us to wonder: why we love; what attracts us to each individual.

We can and do choose to respond to mystery with a sense of wonder and awe. However, we are often a people not at ease with the unknown and the unknowable—and so we respond in fear. Within the church, the fear of homosexuality and homosexual people has cut us off from one another.

That fear has prevented us from seeing into the heart and soul of one an-other. That fear has kept us from loving each other.

To this, the gospel has some very pointed things to say...

Love and fear cannot abide together; "there is no fear in love, but per-fect love casts out fear." Only when we love with the love that is of God will we be released from the fears that keep us separated.

In response to the question, "who is my neighbour?" Jesus tells a par-able wherein the neighbour is the most unlikely person. The one who was seen to be unclean and beyond the reach of God's love turns out to be the bearer of God's love. The gospel commands us to love our neighbour.

Repeatedly, Jesus deliberately identified with the poor, with women and children—the powerless ones of his society. In so doing he demonstrates that God is with these people, calling for and establishing their liberation, in the face of a society that systematically denies them the basic rights and privileges of being human. That same liberating Spirit stirs in the church today—calling for and establishing the liberation of gay and lesbian people ... of all people. The gospel urges us to follow Jesus.

LET'S SPEAK THE TRUTH. LET'S DISPEL THE MYTH THAT ACCUSES HOMOSEXUAL PERSONS OF BEING CHILD MOLESTERS.

If you check history and examine statistics you find that this kind of accusation is simply not true! The truth is children are sexually abused most often by family members of the opposite sex.

LET'S BE CLEAR. HOMOSEXUAL PERSONS ARE NOT INTERESTED IN PERSUADING HETEROSEXUAL PERSONS TO ADOPT THEIR ORIENTATION.

Some people fear that homosexual people want to convince others that their orientation is for everyone. Instead, what is longed for is the realiza-tion that there are faithful lifestyles that differ from the majority. Others fear that if homosexuality is recognized and deemed acceptable, young people will then choose to "become" homosexual people, but people do not "be-come" homosexual through role modelling.

LET'S BE REALISTIC. HOMOSEXUAL PERSONS ARE NOT "OUT THERE TRYING TO GET INTO THE CHURCH."

Many quietly keep the reality of their homosexual orientation a secret, because they are systematically discouraged from revealing their identity, and threatened when they do. Care must be taken when stories or opinions are shared. Justice and understanding are required, not ridicule and verbal abuse. When there are flippant comments about "them," many of "them" are nearby, listening, hoping for neighbourly care, and expecting to continue to offer gifts as part of the church community.

What can we do?

- Read some of the excellent material available on homosexuality, homophobia and heterosexism and mention it to your friends.

- Do not laugh at jokes/comments made at the expense of lesbian/gay people. Indicate that you find these offensive.

- Develop an operating style that respects each person as an independent/ autonomous human being.

- Join Friends of Affirm.

- Make public statements—formal and informal—demanding an end to discrimination of the basis of sexual orientation.

- Expand your understanding of "family" to include a variety of intimate, life-giving relationships.

- Include words such as "lesbian," "gay," "bisexual," "heterosexual," etc. in your vocabulary (and practice saying them without stumbling or blushing).

- Talk with lesbian and gay friends about what actions and attitudes they find oppressive and what actions and attitudes are liberating.

- In "get acquainted" times, ask people about something other than their families. Be imaginative—ask how they like to spend their time, what they like to read, what excited them, etc.

- Wear "Let's Talk" buttons—and be willing to talk.

- Use inclusive language when referring to partners/lifemates/spouses, etc. This allows folk in varieties of relationships to speak about the people with whom they share life without significant risk.

GLOSSARY

Call - The process by which a congregation invites a person to become its minister. A committee made up of representatives from the congregation and presbytery interviews applicants and makes a recommendation to the congregation. The congregation and presbytery then approve the call.

Christian Education (CE) - Children's and adult educational activities within a congregation, including Bible study, Sunday school, mid-week groups and other congregational learning programs. Most congregations have a CE Committee responsible for planning and carrying out these programs.

Church board or council - The governing body of those congregations or pastoral charges in which the Session and stewards have merged into one single structure. Board members usually include committee chairs. Members are elected by the congregation.

Committees - Groups at all levels of the church—congregation, presbytery, Conference and General Council—that carry out the work of the church. There are usually committees in each congregation to deal with areas such as Christian education, outreach or mission, finance and property, stewardship, worship, personnel and pastoral care.

Commissioner - A lay person or member of the order of ministry who is elected to serve as a member of the General Council.

Conference - A regional level of administration within the United Church. There are 13 Conferences in the United Church. Conferences are responsible for oversight of presbyteries and the ordination or commissioning of candidates for the ministry. All clergy within the bounds of Conference and lay people selected by presbyteries meet annually or biennially to conduct the business of the Conference.

Diaconal Minister - A member of the order of ministry (minister) within the United Church who has been commissioned to the diaconal ministry of education, service and pastoral care. Many diaconal ministers serve in chaplaincy and special outreach ministry; others serve as congregational pastors or educators.

Division of Ministry Personnel and Education (MP&E) - One of the administrative units of the national United Church. The work of the Division includes ministry personnel support, advocacy and administration as well as theological education. The work of the Division is guided by a volunteer body with representatives from across the church, as well as volunteer committees. Divisional staff work out of the national office.

Ecumenical Decade - The decade from 1988-1998 was declared "The Ecumenical Decade of Churches in Solidarity with Women in Church and Society" by the World Council of Churches. The United Church of Canada promoted the goals of the Decade, which included affirming the gifts of women and promoting women's leadership.

Elder - A member of a local congregation, of any age, who is elected to provide spiritual leadership in the congregation. Elders serve as members of the board or Session.

General Council - The highest legislative body of the United Church, which meets every two or three years as a full Council. General Council committees and an Executive carry on its work between Councils. Elected representatives from every Conference meet to set policy, decide program initiatives and budget and act on other business of the church.

The Manual - The United Church's book of policy and procedures. It includes the church's bylaws, as well as the Basis of Union—the original founding charter of The United Church of Canada.

Mission and Service Fund - The central fund of the church that supports work in Canada and overseas. Local congregations and individuals contribute money to the fund to support the work of the wider church.

Official board - The governing body of a pastoral charge. The official board is made up of Session (the elders) and stewards, and meets to make decisions at the local congregational level.

Order of Ministry - There is one order of ministry in the United Church made up of ordained and diaconal ministers. United Church of Canada clergy, diaconal or ordained, are referred to as members of the order of ministry.

Ordained Minister - United Church clergy who serve in ministries of word, sacrament and pastoral care.

Petition - A formal request from any member of a United Church court to that court, or a formal request from one level of a court to another. For example, a United Church member may send a petition to the official board of his or her congregation. A congregation might send a petition to presbytery, etc. If a court chooses to transmit it, a petition on an important matter might move all the way from a local congregation to General Council. Unlike resolutions, petitions originate outside the court that is asked to deal with this concern.

Presbytery - A local unit of administration in the United Church, between Conference and pastoral charge levels. There are 94 presbyteries in the United Church with a typical membership of between 20-50 pastoral charges. All clergy are members of presbytery, along with lay people elected by their congregations. Presbyteries may meet monthly or several times a year depending on the region.

Presbyterial - A regional level of organization of the United Church Women, comprised of representatives of UCW groups within the bounds of a presbytery.

Resolution - A motion from a member or committee of a court of the church that asks that court to take a particular action. Unlike petitions, resolutions originate from within the court acting on them.

Session - The body of elected elders within a congregation. Session is responsible for the spiritual life of the membership as well as its mission in the community, and would discuss such matters as worship, outreach, education and pastoral care. The highest elected officer of Session is called the Clerk of Session.

Stewards - The body in a local congregation that is responsible for its financial affairs. (When there is a board structure, finances are managed by a finance committee.) Most congregations also have a stewardship committee responsible for encouraging regular givings of money, time and other resources.

Settlement - Ordained and diaconal ministers are settled (placed) in a pastoral charge or congregation for their first three or more years of ministry. This process is usually called "settlement," and the setting in which they are placed is called their "settlement charge."

United Church Women (UCW)- A study, fellowship and service organization for women in the United Church. Members of the UCW are organized into groups called "units" within local congregations.